OSPREY COMBAT AIRCRAFT • 67

# ISRAELI F-15 EAGLE UNITS IN COMBAT

SERIES EDITOR: TONY HOLMES

OSPREY COMBAT AIRCRAFT • 67

# ISRAELI F-15 EAGLE UNITS IN COMBAT

SHLOMO ALONI

OSPREY
PUBLISHING

**Front cover**

With 30 minutes to go before the ceasefire ending the Lebanon War came into effect at noon on 11 June 1982, Yoram Peled was leading a four-ship formation of Double Tail Squadron F-15s over the Lebanon Valley when he received target vectoring onto two low-flying Syrian MiG-23s from an Israeli Ground Control Unit. A veteran of the October 1973 Yom Kippur War, during which he had flown F-4E Phantom IIs, and with three F-15 kills already to his credit, Peled was anxious to 'make ace' before the conflict ended.

An F-15 pilot since early 1976, Yoram Peled was the eldest son of former IDF/AF commander Beni Peled, whom many considered to be the 'father of the Israeli F-15 force'. He, more than any other serving officer, had pressed for the purchase of the McDonnell Douglas fighter despite stiff opposition from political and military figures who viewed the jet as excessively expensive. Fittingly, Beni Peled's son was now just minutes away from becoming the world's second F-15 ace.

As Yoram Peled raced over the Lebanon Valley in Baz 678, he encountered an unexpected challenge. The two MiG-23s in front of him were flying as low and as fast as he was, thus preventing him from closing to within firing distance of his preferred weapon – the Rafael Python 3 air-to-air missile. Peled was also too far away to use his M61A1 20 mm cannon. The MiG-23s were within range of his AIM-7F missiles, however, although they were outside the temperamental semi-active radar-homing weapon's textbook engagement envelope. Nevertheless, Peled's radar had a solid target acquisition lock on the trailing MiG-23, despite the surrounding ground clutter, so he decided to take a shot. He later recalled;

'On this particular occasion, I had no other alternative but to fire an AIM-7F in lookdown shoot down mode. I launched a Sparrow without thinking that it would hit the target. My luck held, however, as the AAM flew straight and true, striking the MiG-23 in the tail. Pleased with this result, I wasted no time in firing off a second missile, which destroyed the lead jet.'

With these two MiG-23s giving Yoram Peled his fourth and fifth victories, he had now become the world's second F-15 ace (*Cover artwork by Mark Postlethwaite*)

**This book is dedicated to Nili, Tal, Yael and Maya**

First published in Great Britain in 2006 by Osprey Publishing
Midland House, West Way, Botley, Oxford, OX2 0PH
443 Park Avenue South, New York, NY, 10016, USA
E-mail; info@ospreypublishing.com

ISBN 10: 1 84603 047 1
ISBN 13: 978 1 84603 047 5

Edited by Tony Holmes
Page design by Tony & Stuart Truscott
Cover Artwork by Mark Postlethwaite
Aircraft Profiles by Chris Davey
Scale Drawings by Mark Styling
Index by Alan Thatcher
Originated by PPS Grasmere, Leeds, UK
Printed in China through Bookbuilders

06 07 08 09 10   10 9 8 7 6 5 4 3 2 1

For a catalogue of all books published by Osprey please contact:
NORTH AMERICA
Osprey Direct, C/o Random House Distribution Center,
400 Hahn Road, Westminster, MD 21157
E-mail:info@ospreydirect.com

ALL OTHER REGIONS
Osprey Direct UK, P.O. Box 140 Wellingborough, Northants, NN8 2FA, UK
E-mail: info@ospreydirect.co.uk
**www.ospreypublishing.com**

ACKNOWLEDGEMENTS
The author wishes to express his gratitude to F-15 aircrews, maintainers, friends and colleagues who contributed to the production of this volume. Special thanks also to leading Israeli scale modeller Asher Roth, Head of IDF/AF Media Domain Lt Col Israel Tal, Israeli aviation photographer Ofer Zidon, Israeli aviation journalist Danny Shalom, Yehuda Borovik of *BIAF Israel Air & Space Magazine* and to the Israeli Censorship Bureau, which reviewed and approved this title for publication. To save space, as well as to avoid confusion and repetition, no ranks are mentioned in the text. The identification of IDF/AF F-15 units by name, rather than by number as is the usual military custom, is a prerequisite of the Israeli Censorship Bureau.

# CONTENTS

# BAZ ORIGIN

The political situation in the Middle East initially enabled Israel to become the world's first export customer for the McDonnell Douglas F-15 Eagle, and since then the Israeli Defence Force/Air Force (IDF/AF) has been the only foreign operator of all the variants built to date. Over a 23-year period from 1976 to 1999, Israel accepted a total of 50 F-15A/Bs, 31 F-15C/Ds and 25 F-15Is.

The IDF/AF was also the first air arm to engage Soviet-manufactured fighters with the Eagle, in June 1979. And in keeping with the IDF/AF's philosophy of platform versatility, Israeli F-15s were adapted to perform the air-to-ground mission years prior to the service introduction of the multi-role F-15E Strike Eagle with the USAF in 1988.

An Israeli desire to operate F-15s can be traced back to the October 1973 Yom Kippur (Atonement Day) War, which lasted just 19 days, but cost the IDF/AF more than 100 combat aircraft destroyed in action.

French-built jet fighters had provided the IDF/AF with its cutting edge from 1955 to 1969, Dassault's Mystere IVA being synonymous with the October-November 1956 Sinai campaign and its Mirage IIIC becoming the symbol of the IDF/AF's stunning victory during the June 1967 Six Day War. Israeli pilots might have wanted to have been flying the North American F-86 Sabre against Egyptian MiG-15s in 1956 and the McDonnell Douglas F-4E Phantom II against Arab MiG-21s in 1967, but they nevertheless achieved aerial supremacy in their Dassault fighters. As with the future F-15 buy, politics rather than pilot preference dictated the type of aircraft flown by the IDF/AF during the 1950s and 1960s.

Having blocked arms sales to Israel in the past, the US government finally gave permission for it to be supplied with defensive weaponry, including HAWK surface-to-air missile (SAM) batteries, in the early 1960s. Approval was then given for Douglas to fulfill an IDF/AF requirement for a light attack aircraft to replace the elderly Dassault Ouragan and Mystere, as there was simply no suitable French designed

Old and new, and both built in St Louis, Missouri! The IDF/AF's best multi-role combat aircraft prior to the introduction of the F-15 was the F-4E Phantom II, and in this January 1977 image, the crew of Kurnass 141 from No 119 Sqn taxi past Baz 620 and 646 after landing at Tel Nof. This particular Phantom II had claimed two kills in the Yom Kippur War whilst being flown by Moshe Melnik, who would duly score the F-15's first victory on 27 June 1979. With 5.5 Phantom II kills to his credit, Melnik added 3 victories to his tally in the Baz. The air superiority-optimised Baz was not a direct replacement for the multi-role F-4E, and the IDF/AF only found a true successor to the Phantom II in the F-16C/D and F-16I. The F-15 was, and still is, in a class of its own

During the late 1970s the IDF/AF's fleet of Mirage IIICs doubled as 'Red Force' bandits in DACT sessions that were flown in an effort to hone air combat skills for pilots flying F-15s, F-4Es and Kfirs. Typically, 'Red Force' units would conduct 'roadshow' deployments to air bases in order to fly DACT sorties with the resident squadrons, and this photograph was taken at Tel Nof in the late 1970s during just such a visit. With the Mirage IIIC boasting similar performance figures to the MiG-21, 'Red Force' DACT sorties were very important to the F-15 pilots, as their primary opponents at that time were Syrian 'Fishbeds'

and manufactured combat aircraft available. Some 48 A-4H Skyhawks were supplied from December 1967.

Incensed by this deal, the French government had placed an embargo on the future supply of arms to Israel on 2 June 1967. Three days later the IDF/AF's French-built fighters launched the famous pre-emptive strike that saw the outbreak of the Six Day War.

The overwhelming success of the Mirage IIIC in this conflict resulted in considerable export sales success for the delta fighter. Indeed, orders for the Dassault jet more than doubled in the wake of the Six Day War. The IDF/AF did not derive any benefit from the Mirage IIIC's combat exploits, however, as the French embargo remained in place, affecting an Israeli contract for the supply of Mirage 5MJ multi-role jets. The delivery of A-4H Skyhawks was also temporarily suspended as the US government re-evaluated its arms policy in the region following the Six Day War.

Having seen almost 25 per cent of its frontline fighter force destroyed in the conflict, the IDF/AF now found itself unable to make good these losses. Isolated by the western world through trade embargoes, Israel decided to embark upon an indigenous jet fighter programme. The two-phase Raam (Thunder) project covered the local production of the Mirage 5 in Israel as the Raam A and the development of the improved Raam B delta fighter. The former entered IDF/AF service as the Nesher (Vulture) in 1971, whilst the latter became the General Electric J79-powered Kfir (Lion Cub) fighter, which made its frontline debut in 1975.

US trade restrictions were soon lifted, and IDF/AF service personnel welcomed the shift from French to American equipment, as hardware from the latter source was generally superior – especially in respect to avionics, powerplants and weapon systems. This technology came at a price, however, as the US government has always viewed the export of weapons to Israel as a tool of diplomacy in the Middle East. For the past 40 years this has meant that the IDF/AF has had to tailor its operational requirements to suit American willingness to supply it with aircraft.

While the US government complied with its pre-Six Day War contract to supply F-4E Phantom IIs to Israel from 1969 as an alternative to the embargoed Mirage 5MJs, ongoing deliveries could only be assured if American diplomatic goals could be achieved in the region. Unhappy with this proviso to any future deals, and in light of the French embargo, Israel pressed ahead with its indigenous jet fighter projects.

In 1969 the Israeli Ministry of Defence directed the IDF/AF to outline the operational requirement for a fighter that would succeed the F-4E and

Moti Hod (right) handed over command of the IDF/AF to Beni Peled (left) on 10 May 1973. Hod, who had been in charge of the air force since 1966, received great praise in Israel for his leadership skills during the June 1967 Six Day War. In contrast to Hod, Peled courted controversy during his time in charge of the IDF/AF. He was a strong believer in 'responsibility-authority', which meant that a commander could only be held responsible for the actions that took place within the jurisdiction of his immediate command. In the wake of the October 1973 Yom Kippur War, Peled restructured the IDF/AF so that it better reflected his 'responsibility-authority' dictum. A staunch supporter of the F-15 and F-16 High-Low fighter mix, and a bitter opponent of Israel's indigenous combat aircraft projects, Peled commanded the IDF/AF until October 1977

the Raam B in service in the 1980s. Beni Peled, who headed the IDF/AF's Air Department from 1971 until 1973, duly created a team to evaluate future fighter designs under the codename Team Hadish (Modern).

## IMMEDIATE THREAT

As Team Hadish was trying to define the IDF/AF operational requirements for the 1980s, Egypt and Israel clashed again. No diplomatic solution had been reached at the end of the Six Day War, with Egypt's President Abdel Gamal El-Nasser publicly announcing soon afterwards that 'what had been taken by force will be returned by force'. This statement was further reinforced on 1 September 1967 when Arab leaders adopted the 'Three Nos' policy at the Khartoum Summit – No recognition of Israel, No negotiation with Israel and No peace.

In light of this diplomatic dead-end in the region, limited-scale hostilities continued in the wake of the Six Day War. Perhaps the most significant lesson learned by the Arab countries during the June 1967 conflict was that their fighter pilots, flying Soviet aircraft and employing Soviet tactics, were no match for their Israeli counterparts. Chastened by their losses, the Egyptians and Syrians now decided to challenge the superiority of the IDF/AF not from the air but from the ground.

The first step in this direction came in 1968, when the Egyptians created an Air Defence Force (ADF) to protect their airspace. With help from the USSR, they would rapidly establish a network of SAM sites, overlapping in coverage and protected by anti-aircraft artillery (AAA) and newly-delivered MiG-21 interceptors. These sites would also be supported by control centres and radar stations.

Confident in the capabilities of the restructured Egyptian armed forces, President El-Nasser launched the War of Attrition in March 1969. By early 1970 Israel had secured an advantage in this principally static conflict, which was fought along a 160-kilometre front west of the Suez Canal. Following a series of pin-point strikes on key ADF sites, the SAM threat crumbled, allowing Israeli F-4Es to attack strategic targets all over Egypt virtually unchallenged. Yet despite the reduction in its ability to wage a war of attrition, the Egyptian leadership refused to terminate hostilities without having first achieved some kind of military victory.

Countering the attacks being made by the F-4Es was seen by President Nasser as the key to Egyptian success, so he made an emergency visit to Moscow in late January 1970. Once in the USSR, he persuaded his hosts that the only way to avoid another humiliating defeat for Soviet technology was through direct communist intervention.

There were already 1500 Soviet advisors in Egypt at the time, and every regiment-sized military unit in the country had at least one Russian within its ranks – several had also been killed in the war to date. In the wake of President Nasser's visit, these advisors were joined by a complete Soviet ADF division, which included an integrated MiG-21 air brigade.

Equipped with AAA, radar stations, command & control facilities and the latest versions of the SA-2 and SA-3 SAMs, the Soviet division initially assumed responsibility for the defence of Alexandria, Cairo and the Aswan Dam. The deployment of the Soviet division in turn freed up hard-pressed Egyptian ADF units to engage the IDF/AF in the battle for air superiority west of the Suez Canal.

Thanks to the introduction of the latest Soviet technology, operated by Soviet troops, the balance of power swung in favour of the Egyptian ADF. By mid-1970, SAMs had downed five F-4Es and badly damaged two more. These losses proved the new-found effectiveness of the Egyptian-Soviet Integrated Air Defence System (IADS) west of the Suez Canal.

By the time the undeclared War of Attrition ended in August 1970, thanks to a US-brokered peace deal, the success of the Egyptian-Soviet IADS had given President Nasser the victory that he had sought in order to accept a ceasefire agreement. However, the latter was fragile, and both sides prepared for the resumption of hostilities at any time, as none of the basic issues that had triggered the conflict had been resolved.

Having suffered such losses to the ADF, the Israelis were keen to monitor the proliferation of SAM sites in Sinai and Egypt. Unable to fly over the IADS, the IDF/AF needed a platform capable of Long-Range Oblique Photography (LOROP) from the safety of Israeli airspace.

Conversely, the Egyptians had no such problems monitoring IDF movements east of the border, as they had direct access to intelligence data collected by Soviet MiG-25R 'Foxbat-B' reconnaissance aircraft that began flying missions from Egyptian bases from March 1971. IDF/AF F-4E crews attempted to intercept the high and fast MiG-25Rs, but the Phantom II was no match for the Soviet aircraft.

Clearly an interceptor superior to the F-4E was needed to intercept the 'Foxbat-B', but none existed at the time. The only option available to the IDF/AF was to improve the Phantom II's rate of climb and top-end speed, so the Israeli Technion Institute of Technology's Jet Engines Laboratory commenced a study into the application of Pre-Compressor Cooling (PCC) so as to increase the thrust of the fighter's J79 turbojets.

The threat posed by the MiG-25 was not unique to Israel, and the USAF had already contracted General Dynamics to develop a PCC Phantom II, known unofficially as the F-4X project, in conjunction with McDonnell Douglas. In order to allow the equipment associated with PCC to be installed in the airframe of the F-4, extensive modifications had to be carried out to the jet's air intakes. Two water tanks were duly bolted onto the airframe above the intakes, each tank having the capacity to hold 2500-US gallons of water. These tanks also featured self-contained systems that included all the necessary pumping equipment so as to avoid further structural modifications having to be made to the jet.

Water sprayed into the air inlets from the tanks increased the mass of the airflow into the engine, thus boosting thrust at high speed and high altitude by 150 per cent. Although the PCC tanks added drag and weight, the performance gains expected were big enough to offset these penalties.

The F-4X was designed to achieve dash speeds of Mach 3.2 and cruise at Mach 2.4. Although such performance figures might have allowed it to intercept the MiG-25R, the existence of the F-4X threatened the future of a major USAF project that was expressly designed to counter the 'Foxbat'. McDonnell Douglas' F-15 Eagle was only three years away from entering service with the USAF at the time development work was being carried out on the F-4X. Nothing could be allowed to divert funding from this programme, so the USAF withdrew its support for the F-4X.

Realising that it could only dream of an early F-15 purchase, the IDF/AF pinned its hopes on the F-4X to such a degree that it provided funds to the project, as well as a precious F-4E to serve as a mock-up. With the USAF's abandonment of the project, Israel could not afford to payroll the F-4X, so it turned its attention once again to the F-15.

The F-4 had entered IDF/AF service some eight years after it had first been fielded by the US military. Based on a similar timeline, the soonest the Israelis could expect to acquire the F-15 was in the early 1980s. With France sticking firmly to its trade embargo, and US arms sales to Israel predicated on the state of diplomatic relations between the two countries, and their Arab neighbours, at the time, the IDF/AF appeared to have little option but to back the development of a home-grown fighter.

By the early 1970s, the Raam A had metamorphosed into the Israeli Aircraft Industries (IAI) Nesher and entered frontline service. The development of the Raam B was also well underway, with IDF/AF service entry planned for early 1974. Neither machine could intercept a MiG-25R or match the performance of the F-15, however. The obvious next step was to develop a Raam B successor, and IAI duly started producing preliminary design studies for an Israeli jet for the 1980s.

Senior officers in the IDF/AF quickly realised that an indigenous design that was locally produced would struggle to achieve parity with western fighters because the aircraft would have to rely on a foreign-built powerplant and sub-systems rendered unavailable by the French arms embargo and/or the vagaries of US foreign policy. As a result of these delays, IAI estimated that it would take at least ten years to develop a Raam B replacement from scratch. With little prospect of the Israeli fighter entering service before the mid-1980s, Team Hadish was explicitly against the development of an indigenous Raam B successor.

The team instead reiterated the fact that the IDF/AF had to persist in its efforts to purchase the F-15 or, alternatively, Grumman's F-14 Tomcat – the latter had entered service with the US Navy in late 1972. Both projects were duly presented to an Israeli delegation, led by Head of the Air Department Beni Peled, during a visit to the USA in August 1972.

On 4 October 1973, the IDF's General Headquarters held a meeting with staff officers working on the future fighter procurement programme to check on what progress had been made to date. Two days later, Egypt and Syria launched a coordinated surprise attack on Israel to mark the start of the 19-day offensive that became known as the Yom Kippur War. This campaign ultimately hastened the arrival of the IDF/AF's next fighter by eight years.

Although lasting less than three weeks, the Yom Kippur War proved to be a painful experience for Israeli aircrew. The success of Egypt's ADF in the War of Attrition had shown that IADS would play a major part in any future conflict in the area, and this proved to be the case in October 1973.

By the mid-1970s air-to-air kill scoreboards like this one adorned the walls of IDF/AF fighter squadrons. Most of these kills were credited to Mirage IIIC and F-4 crews, and the vast percentage of the aircraft destroyed were MiG-21s. The Soviet jet had a similar performance to both the French and American fighters, but was thoroughly outclassed by the F-15. The latter aircraft had been acquired in order to establish a long-lasting technological gap between Israeli interceptors and Arab fighters, and the Baz was well suited to this role. Just how well suited is clearly revealed by this photograph of the Double Tail Squadron's scoreboard, which records each of the 45.5 kills that were credited to the unit between 1979 and 1982. It is true that several ex-Mirage IIIC and F-4 squadrons have higher victory tallies, but only the F-15 community could boast that it has never lost an aircraft in aerial combat

In the Six Day War, the IDF/AF had claimed 452 Arab aircraft destroyed for the loss of just 46 aeroplanes, thus giving Israeli pilots a claims-to-losses ratio of 10-to-1. This ratio had dropped sharply to 4-to-1 by the end of the Yom Kippur War, when the IDF/AF claimed the destruction of 433 aircraft for the loss of 109 Israeli aeroplanes.

On average, the IDF/AF downed 75 aircraft per day during the conflict in June 1967, but this figure had decreased to 23 during the Yom Kippur War. These statistics reveal the effectiveness of the IDF/AF overall, because it has always suffered from numerical inferiority when compared with its enemies. Had the IDF/AF been able to maintain its claims-to-losses ratio from the Six Day War in October 1973, the 19-day conflict may very well have been drastically shortened, thus resulting in less of a drain on precious Israeli resources.

There were two principal reasons why the IDF/AF had proven less effective in the Yom Kippur War. Firstly, it had failed to act as a suitable deterrent against Arab aggression, despite its impressive performance in the Six Day War. This was primarily because of the losses it had suffered in the latter stages of the War of Attrition, when the Egyptians had seen that the IDF/AF was unable to properly contain its IADS threat.

Secondly, a next generation fighter aircraft was clearly required to boost the claims-to-losses ratio back to 1967 levels. The F-4E, MiG-21 and Mirage IIIC were all comparable platforms, so the IDF/AF had to rely on its battle-proven tactics and training as the decisive factors in combat. However, the superior quality of its pilots was no longer enough when up against SAMs and fighters operating as part of a modern IADS.

By the end of the Yom Kippur War, it was clear to Israeli politicians and senior military personnel alike that the only way the IDF/AF was going to improve its kill-to-loss ratio, and thus deter future Arab aggression, was to obtain at least a squadron's worth of next generation fighters.

## DIPLOMATIC BREAKTHROUGH

The primary focus of US Cold War diplomacy during the early 1970s was to put an end to regional conflicts, as successive administrations in the White House understood that 'local' wars could potentially escalate into a direct conflict between the two superpowers. Undoubtedly the 'hottest' of all 'hot spots' during this period was the Middle East, and the Americans were squarely behind the United Nations (UN) when it imposed a ceasefire that ended the Yom Kippur War on 24 October 1973. By then, Arab advances had been repulsed by the IDF, and its Forward Line of Troops (FLOT) was within artillery range of Damascus in the northeast, and 100 kilometres from Cairo in the west.

Despite IDF advances on the Egyptian-Israeli front, both sides were occupying land that they had not previously held pre-war. Therefore, the UN placed its highest priority on stabilising the border in Sinai. The US government, through the auspices of the UN, exerted pressure on the Israelis to pull back from the Suez Canal's west bank so that a proper buffer zone could be created between the opposing armies. A clearly defined FLOT was essential if a the ceasefire was to be enforced.

A UN-brokered disengagement agreement was duly signed by Egypt and Israel on 18 January 1974, and troops from both sides had completed their pull out from occupied territories by March. A second disengagement agreement between Egypt and Israel was signed on 4 September 1975, providing for further Israeli withdrawals (that were completed by February 1976) and the creation of a larger buffer zone under UN Emergency Force II control.

As part of the agreement that enabled Israel to pull back, the US government guaranteed that the IDF would subsequently enjoy a significant technological edge. The cornerstone of this military 'insurance package' was permission for Israel to introduce a new fighter into service far sooner than could have been expected prior to the Yom Kippur War and the 1974-75 disengagement agreements.

The IDF/AF formulated a requirement for 50 next generation fighters, and in June 1974 Israeli Ministry of Defence Shimon Peres forwarded a request to evaluate the two main candidates. Permission was granted in light of the recently achieved disengagement, and a large Israeli delegation, including IDF/AF and IAI test pilots and engineers, arrived in the USA in September. The delegation's mandate was simple – to evaluate and then recommend which fighter (the F-14 or the F-15) was more suited to fulfil the IDF/AF requirement.

Israeli pilots had flown both fighter types prior to the official evaluation. Indeed, IDF/AF commander (from 1973 to 1977) Beni Peled had been one of the first non-Americans to fly an Eagle when he piloted a pre-production TF-15 from the front seat during a visit to Edwards AFB in 1974. Peled had been impressed with the visibility on offer from the jet's cockpit, but otherwise he could not rate the combat potential of the F-15, as the aircraft he was flying was still very much a development airframe that lacked operational mission equipment.

David Ivry, who headed up the IDF/AF's Air Department/Group from 1973 to 1975, had flown an F-14 from Naval Air Station (NAS) Miramar during a visit to the USA in early 1974. The sortie involved several Dissimilar Air Combat Training (DACT) scenarios against an A-4 Skyhawk flown by an adversary squadron. Ivry later recalled;

'I was impressed with the F-14, even though it was heavy on the controls. The aircraft's engines were also sensitive, which meant that it was impossible to fly the Tomcat as aggressively as we would our jets.'

By the time Ivry made his flight in the F-14, the jet had already been chosen by Iran instead of the F-15. At this time Iran was an Israeli ally that was faced with the same threats from neighbouring Iraq and the USSR – including overflights by MiG-25R/RBs. The Iranians had evaluated the F-14 and the F-15 in 1973, and had duly become the first export customer for a US 'teen' series fighter when it signed a contract for the Tomcat in June 1974. Three months later it was the turn of the Israelis to evaluate the two air superiority fighters.

Amnon Arad headed up the team sent to test the aircraft. An ex-F-4 squadron CO, he was in fact heading Team Hadish when he was given the opportunity to evaluate the F-14 and F-15. Arad was, at that time, the only fighter pilot in the team, so three more joined just prior to the mission leaving Israel. Israel Baharav represented the Mirage III/ Nesher community, Omri Afek, like Arad, was an F-4 pilot and Assaf Ben-Nun was IAI's Kfir Project Test Pilot.

These four pilots had a combined total of 24 victories between them, with Baharav and Ben-Nun being aces with twelve and five credited

IDF/AF F-14 and F-15 evaluation pilots pose with McDonnell Douglas test pilots in front of an F-15 prototype in 1974. Amnon Arad is standing second from left, while the kneeling pilots are (from left to right) Israel Baharav, Assaf Ben-Nun and Omri Afek

kills, respectively. Other members of the team included F-4 navigator Aharon Katz and IAI and IDF/AF engineers. Included amongst the latter was Moshe Keret, who was IAI's Lahav Plant managing director in charge of fighter production – he later became IAI President and Chief Executive Officer from 1985 to 2006.

The purpose of the evaluation was to examine the merits of the two new generation fighters in three scenarios based on lessons learned from the Yom Kippur War. The team would test how the jets went about achieving air superiority over the battlefield, as well as evaluating their ability to intercept a wide variety of targets from low and slow helicopters to high and fast MiG-25s, as well as high-speed attack aircraft flying at low altitude and Tu-16 bombers armed with long-range air-to-surface missiles. Finally, the fighters' ability to escort IDF/AF formations on long-range missions would also be examined.

Although the F-14 and F-15 had been developed over a similar timeframe, they differed in concept. The Tomcat was designed to defend US Navy carrier battlegroups, while the Eagle had been built specifically to challenge enemy aircraft over the battlefield. The F-14 was a two-seat weapon system, while the F-15 was a single-seat fighter.

The latter machine appeared to address the IDF/AF's principal operational requirements, and the Israelis therefore expected the F-15 to be the better air superiority platform – the F-14 had been developed almost exclusively as an interceptor. Nevertheless, both jets could fly far and fight with minimal ground control unit (GCU) inputs.

This performance came at a high price, however, and aside from reporting on the aircrafts' mission capabilities, the evaluation team was also to submit recommendations in respect to the economics of purchase, and the long term costs involved in operating the rival jets.

The IDF/AF requested a head-to-head evaluation in order to compare the F-14 and F-15, but US government approval was not granted for such a fly-off. Instead, the evaluation team prepared a series of mission profiles that saw the aircraft up against the A-4 and the F-4.

Israeli pilots flew the Eagle first in a series of nine flights from the McDonnell Douglas plant in St Louis, Missouri. A different scenario was evaluated in each sortie, and all were flown in a two-seat TF-15A Full-Scale Development (FSD) airframe that had an Israeli pilot strapped into the front seat and a US test pilot in the back. One of the flights simulated the interception of a high and fast MiG-25, whilst in another the TF-15 easily 'shot down' an F-4 flown by Omri Afek.

The Israelis were very impressed by the view from the TF-15's cockpit, as well as the jet's thrust-to-weight ratio. Its harmonised weapon system, which enabled both within visual range (WVR) and beyond visual range (BVR) engagements to be conducted with ease, also drew praise.

Assaf Ben-Nun flew two sorties in TF-15A 71-0290, the first lasting 55 minutes (he had McDonnell Douglas test pilot J E Krings in the back seat) and the second 45 minutes (flown with company test pilot D D Behm). Ben-Nun recalled;

'I was an IAI employee and an IDF/AF reserve pilot when I joined the evaluation team as a test pilot following a direct request by IDF/AF commander Beni Peled. We initially "flew" the two F-15 simulators – the

cockpit simulator and the air combat simulator, the latter housed in two domes – and they were both exceptionally realistic.

'In my first TF-15 flight, I successfully practised a BVR interception scenario with a semi-active radar-homed (SARH) air-to-air missile (AAM), then a WVR scenario with both an infrared (IR) AAM and the cannon. Both attacks were successfully made during a solitary pass against my opponent. Performance-wise, the F-15 was a revelation, with superb acceleration and manoeuvrability. My only reservation centred on its large size, as I preferred smaller fighters for air combat.'

The IDF/AF's evaluation of the F-14 at NAS Miramar was undertaken in such a way as to check whether the aircraft could match the F-15's performance, rather than better it. From an Israeli point of view, the Tomcat could not match the three principal virtues of the Eagle – the F-14 had a framed rather than a bubble canopy, its thrust-to-weight ratio was significantly inferior to the F-15's and the Grumman jet's weapon system was optimised for BVR scenarios.

Israel Baharav was intimately involved in the evaluation of the F-14, and he later recalled;

'The IDF/AF has always labelled its most modern fighter "superior" and the previous generation jet "inferior". For example, the Super Mystere was superior to the Mystere up until the Mirage IIIC entered service, when both became inferior to the Dassault delta. Typically, the

**About to conduct an evaluation flight, 12-kill Mirage IIIC ace Israel Baharav is handed his flying helmet soon after climbing into the cockpit of a TF-15A at St Louis in September 1974**

**Project *Peace Fox II* covered the delivery of nine brand new F-15Cs (USAF 80-0122 to 80-0130) and six F-15Ds (USAF serials 80-0131 to 80-0136) in 1981-82. The arrival of the first *Peace Fox II* jets coincided with the delivery of the F-16A/Bs that had been temporarily held in the USA following the Israeli strike on Iraq's Osirak nuclear reactor on 7 June 1981. F-15D 80-0131 led the first three *Peace Fox II* jets into Tel Nof on 25 August 1981, along with F-15C 80-0122 and F-15D 80-0132. This photograph was taken immediately after their arrival in Israel**

*Peace Fox IV* deliveries of five F-15Ds (USAF serials 90-0275 to 90-0279) commenced on 4 May 1992 when the first two Baz 4s landed at Tel Nof. By then the USAF had adopted 'low viz' paint schemes for its F-15s, and the aircraft built for Israel were also camouflaged accordingly. In line with a long-standing IDF/AF tradition, flowers are about to be presented to the crew that has ferried this jet (F-15D 90-0275) in from St Louis

The first Baz 5s were actually delivered before the Baz 4s simply because they were secondhand A/B-models drawn from USAF stocks. The first of these aircraft landed at Tel Nof on 23 October 1991, and included in their ranks was F-15A 74-0122, which ended its useful life as a donator of parts for the rebuild of Baz 689

IDF/AF usually found that although the superior fighter had a better thrust-to-weight ratio, the inferior fighter was more agile. When performing DACT between superior and inferior fighters, the pilot flying the latter must strive to make the fight a turning engagement, while his opponent has to preserve a high-energy state.

'During our evaluation of the F-14 and F-15 against the F-4 and A-4, we stuck firmly to the principles of the superior fighter versus the inferior jet. We prepared ourselves accordingly, and were thoroughly familiar with the performance statistics associated with all four aircraft. We instinctively figured that the F-14 and F-15 would carry more energy coming into the fight, but that they would turn more slowly than the A-4 in particular.

'Despite our preparations, we were simply amazed when we flew the F-15 against the F-4. The Eagle maintained it thrust-to-weight advantage and turned much quicker than the F-4. Here we had a superior fighter that was also more manoeuvrable than the inferior jet!

'When we evaluated the F-14, the US Navy pilots at NAS Miramar told us that the Tomcat could perform equally as well in a dogfight with an A-4. This did not prove to be the case, however, for when I flew the TA-4 against the F-14, the end result of the engagement was embarrassment for the Tomcat. Not only could the TA-4 out-turn the F-14, but during the turn itself, the Tomcat's energy state dropped so low that I was able to fly the TA-4 in the vertical as though the Skyhawk was the superior fighter and the F-14 the inferior!'

Assaf Ben-Nun also flew a two-hour sortie in a TA-4F that included DACT against the F-14, and he too was disappointed to discover that the Skyhawk was superior to the F-14 in the WVR air combat scenario. He then flew a one-hour Tomcat mission from Naval Air

Facility El Centro, in California, with US Navy pilot Keith Sheehan in the back seat. Ben-Nun remembered;

'The F-14 lacked thrust, was complex and not user-friendly and was not aerodynamically clean – indeed, the jet shuddered every time I pulled high-G or high angle-of-attack. During my sortie, I flew DACT against Amnon Arad in a Skyhawk, and although we finished with honours even at the end of the session, I found it hard to believe that the F-14 had no edge whatsoever over the A-4 in WVR air combat.'

The Israelis acknowledged that cockpit teamwork between the pilot and his Radar Intercept Officer might go some way to narrowing the gap between the two jets. Conversely, the evaluation team stated that the Tomcat's ability to simultaneously intercept several targets at very long range was mostly irrelevant to Middle East air warfare scenarios.

Overall, the F-15 clearly emerged as the better fighter for the IDF/AF. Technologically, it was judged to be the more advanced jet, and it was also expected to have better growth potential. The latter view has proven to have been the correct one, for 30 years later the F-15 is still in low-rate production, but the F-14 has now been withdrawn from US Navy service. Furthermore, the Tomcat was more expensive than the Eagle, and it was expected to project significantly higher service life costs. The purchase of 50 F-14s would have cost the Israeli government $870 million, as opposed to $628 million for an identical number of F-15s. The evaluation team estimated the direct operating costs at $1689 per flight hour for the F-14 and $1073 for the F-15. The F-15 emerged as the clear winner both on the grounds of performance and cost, and the IDF/AF happily accepted the verdict.

Selection of the F-15 was a milestone in the IDF/AF's procurement of the aircraft, but with Israel still recovering from a costly war, the country's economy was at a low ebb after months of mobilisation. And although investment in the nation's defence was the government's highest priority, the purchase of such a costly aircraft was openly questioned as, ironically, air superiority had been the only area in which the IDF/AF had excelled during the Yom Kippur War. Control of the skies had failed to deter the Arabs from invading Israel, however.

It was against this background that the IDF/AF went on the political offensive in an effort to secure funding for the purchase of the F-15. In the 'frontline' of the battle were the various members of the September 1974 evaluation team, including Israel Baharav, who had been assigned to the IDF/AF's Weapon Systems Department as the F-15 Project Officer upon his return from the USA. He recalled;

'IDF/AF commander Beni Peled ordered me to join him for a meeting with the Minister of Defence to discuss the F-15 – I was to outline the jet's virtues as an air superiority platform. Despite my best efforts, Minister of Defence Shimon Peres was not impressed with my presentation, which centred on explaining how the F-4 was inferior to the F-15. Both aircraft had an armament of four IR AAMs and four SARH AAMs, both were twin-engined and both had similar top speeds. I was therefore asking him to fund the purchase of 50 $50 million jets on the premise that the F-15 was considerably more manoeuvrable and had a much better radar, with a look-down shoot down capability, than the F-4.

'Then the Minister asked, "Can the F-4 fly a mission to the Straits of Bab El-Mandab and back without in-flight refuelling?" "No" was my answer, so he asked, "Can the F-15 fly such a mission?" I answered "Yes, but . . ." and I asked him if I could present him with a feasibility study in two months – the Minister gave us two weeks. I duly returned a fortnight later with a map and a range circle for a high-low-high sortie profile, with the F-15 carrying two bombs and completing the mission without in-flight refuelling. This was enough to convince the government to buy the world's best air superiority fighter, based on the jet's air-to-ground attack potential!'

In early December 1974 the US government officially offered Israel 48 F-15s for delivery from late 1975 onwards at a rate of two jets per month. And although successful diplomacy in the region had given the IDF/AF the opportunity to evaluate the F-14 and F-15, select the latter as its fighter of choice and to accept an offer to purchase the aircraft, the actual delivery of these jets was still wholly dependent on the political situation between Israel and its Arab neighbours.

When second disengagement negotiations between Egypt and Israel became bogged down in March 1975, President Gerald Ford's administration announced a reassessment of the US relationship with Israel. As a result of the latter, the IDF/AF F-15 purchase process was suspended until the second disengagement agreement between Egypt and Israel was finally signed on 4 September 1975.

Within weeks the US government had agreed to supply Israel with 25 F-15s in a contract totalling $625 million. In an effort to speed up the delivery of these aircraft, the Americans offered to include a substantial number of refurbished FSD jets ahead of new-build airframes. The IDF/AF was reluctant to agree to the purchase of refurbished F-15s, but the Israeli government was anxious for an accelerated delivery of these aircraft before the US administration changed its mind once again. Finally, a compromise was reached whereby four refurbished F-15A FSDs would be delivered in late 1976, followed by 19 F-15As and two TF-15A two-seaters (the designation was changed to F-15B in October 1978) from McDonnell Douglas' St Louis production line from late 1977 onwards.

Finally, in January 1976, a modest $15.2 million contract awarded to McDonnell Douglas by the US Department of Defense to cover the refurbishment of four FSD jets got the Israeli Project *Peace Fox* F-15 purchase process underway.

The delivery of surplus USAF F-15s to Israel in the early 1990s as part of Project *Peace Fox V* meant that the IDF/AF could eventually retire one of the more weary jets supplied to act as a gate guard at the entrance of Tel Nof air base. Stripped of all useable spare parts, F-15A 73-0107 was then marked up as fictitious 'Baz 008' (complete with Syrian kill markings) and adorned with the name *Tel Nof* in Hebrew script on the nose. The fighter was put on display near the base's main gate in 2005

The four FSD airframes sold to Israel were 72-0116, 72-0117, 72-0118 and 72-0120, and these became Baz 620, 622, 644 and 646 respectively. The first *Peace Fox* project also covered the supply of 19 F-15As (76-1505 to 76-1523) and two F-15Bs (76-1524 and 76-1525). 72-0117 was photographed upon its late arrival at Tel Nof on 10 December 1976

# DOUBLE TAIL SQUADRON

Eitan Ben-Eliyahu had graduated as part of the IDF/AF's Flying School Class 44 in 1964, after which he had flown Ouragans until late 1967, when he converted to the Mirage IIICJ. In 1969 Ben-Eliyahu attended the F-4 Conversion Course Class 1, and the Phantom II would be his mount for the next seven years. During this time he completed a USAF Fighter Weapons School course and commanded an F-4 squadron between 13 October 1973 and 27 January 1976. His combat record included a single aerial victory in the Mirage IIIC and two in the F-4. A gifted leader, Ben-Eliyahu was chosen to lead the F-15 Set-Up Team and to command the IDF/AF's first F-15 squadron.

Aside from Ben-Eliyahu, the four other pilots chosen to man the Set-Up Team were selected because of their vast fast jet experience. Benny Zinker had graduated from Flying School Class 53 in 1967 and flown armed Fouga Magister trainers during the Six Day War whilst still an air cadet. He then attended the Ouragan Operational Training Unit (OTU) and saw frontline service in the Mystere, F-4 and A-4. Moshe Melnik was a graduate of Flying School Class 54 in 1967, and following his spell with the Ouragan OTU, he flew A-4s and F-4s in squadron service.

The final two members of the team were Yoel Feldsho and Shaul Simon. The former had previously flown the Sud-Ouest Vautour, Mirage IIIC and F-4, while the latter had recently finished a tour on Phantom IIs – Simon was also the son of an IDF/AF B-17 Flying Fortress navigator.

The five pilots headed to America in July 1976, where they attended a USAF F-15 conversion course during IDF/AF Year 1976 Term 2. The four refurbished F-15 FSD airframes that they would soon fly, meanwhile, were due for delivery at the beginning of IDF/AF 1976 Term 3. The IDF/AF's year, which coincided with the Israeli fiscal year that ran from the 1 April until 31 March, was divided into three terms – Term 1, from April to July, Term 2, from August to November, and Term 3, from December to March.

To familiarise themselves with USAF procedures, Set-Up Team pilots attended an Advanced Instrument School course at Randolph AFB, Texas, prior to commencing the F-15 conversion course at Luke AFB, Arizona. The Israeli pilots flew their first solo flights in the Eagle on 30 September 1976, and completed F-15 course F1500F with the

The Double Tail Squadron's Set-Up Team pose for the camera during the FY 1976 Term 2 conversion course staged at Luke AFB – note the unit emblem on their helmets. These pilots are, from left to right, Shaul Simon, Benny Zinker, Moshe Melnik, Yoel Feldsho and Eitan Ben-Eliyahu. A combined total of 12 MiGs would be destroyed by these pilots between June 1979 and June 1982. TF-15A 73-0111 parked behind them is painted in an experimental Ferris scheme that was trialled on this jet in 1977

USAF's 555th Tactical Fighter Training Squadron as members of Class 76 AFL on 15 November 1976. Upon completion of the conversion course, they visited McDonnell Douglas in St Louis, Missouri, to learn more about the F-15's avionics and features.

The Israeli F-15s were similar to those flown by the USAF except for a few minor modifications that would allow them to be armed with locally-built AAMs then under development – principally the Rafael Python 3, which entered IDF/AF service in 1978. The IDF/AF also requested that the jet's avionics be modified so that the pilot could automatically range-trigger shift the displays on his radar screens, as well as updating the inertial navigation system (INS) waypoints in exactly the same way.

## THE FIRST FOUR

The IDF/AF's first F-15 unit, known as the Double Tail Squadron, was activated at Tel Nof on 28 November 1976. Its establishment came at the beginning of IDF/AF Year 1976 Term 3, and was followed shortly after by the departure of a second group of five Israeli pilots to the USA to undertake the F-15 conversion course.

This group consisted of Avner Naveh, Yoram Peled, Alex Gan, Ram Caller and Guy Golan. Naveh had graduated from Flying School Class 64 in 1971 and then flown the Ouragan whilst at the OTU, followed by the Super Mystere, prior to converting onto the F-4 in 1972. Peled had been a graduate of Flying School Class 66, also in 1971, and had flown the A-4 in the frontline after mastering the Ouragan during his time with the OTU. He too had converted onto F-4s in IDF/AF Year 1972 Term 3.

When asked about his training in the USA, Peled recalled;

'We followed in the footsteps of the first five pilots to make the conversion. It started with the Advanced Instrument School course on T-38s at Randolph AFB, as senior officers in the IDF/AF wanted to make sure that all F-15 pilots were capable of flying the aircraft effectively in all weather conditions. My father, who was commander of the IDF/AF at the time, firmly believed that in order for fighter pilots to be able to perform their mission properly, they had to be proficient at flying on instruments too. He would often recall how well he had been served throughout his career by the RAF instrument flying course he had completed in the UK in the early 1950s, prior to converting onto jets.'

With five F-15-rated pilots in Israel, and five more undergoing their conversion in the USA, the Double Tail Squadron was ready to accept the first four F-15A FSD jets by late 1976 – USAF pilots duly ferried them to Israel, using the IDF/AF codename Operation *Kartiv* (Ice Lolly) *1*.

The scheduled arrival date was Friday, 10 December 1976, and the estimated time of arrival (ETA) was 1500 hrs local time – later than was usual for an official government ceremony. Governing a Jewish State, the Israeli government goes to great lengths to avoid scheduling official ceremonies during the Sabbath, which is in effect from Friday afternoon through to Saturday evening. The long flight from the USA to Israel could only be achieved with two in-flight refuellings en route, and with an ETA of 1500 hrs local time, even the shortest of delays in the transatlantic crossing would see the ceremony clash with the start of the Sabbath.

The ETA came and went without any sign of the jets, or any radio communication to update IDF/AF officials on their arrival. When Israeli air traffic controllers did finally establish contact, they were notified that three of the jets were still 45 minutes away from Tel Nof – the fourth F-15 had had to land in Italy due to a technical malfunction. This in flight emergency, combined with headwinds and in-flight refuelling difficulties, had delayed the aircraft.

By then it was obvious that the actual ETA would result in the ceremony creeping into the Sabbath, which resulted in a few guests hastily leaving the air base. Most of the guests, including Israeli Prime Minister Yitzhak Rabin, remained at Tel Nof to welcome the jets, however. And once the ceremony finally got underway, IDF Chief of Staff Mordechai Gur said in his speech 'Israel and the IDF with the F-15 are a different nation and a different army'.

Mordechai Gur's comments were indeed prophetic, but in a most unexpected way. The following evening, the National Religious Party announced its withdrawal from the Labor Party coalition government. Its official statement explained that it could no longer support a government that officially celebrated the F-15s' arrival during the Sabbath. Without the support of the National Religious Party, the Labor Party government collapsed. The National Likud Party won the ensuing elections in 1977, thus ending 29 years of Labor Party government. Cynics immediately announced that the collapse of the Labor Party government was the F-15's first kill!

Away from the political fall-out associated with the arrival of the F-15s, the five pilots assigned to the Double Tail Squadron started working towards initial operational capability with the jets at Tel Nof. Initially, the F-15s, the pilots and the maintainers all shared a single hardened aircraft shelter (HAS) complex that was known as the Interception HAS.

And by then, the aircraft assigned to the unit were no longer just F-15s, as the IDF/AF had allocated the Hebrew name Baz (Buzzard) to the fourth generation jet fighter.

**Below**
**Baz 646 (F-15A 72-0120) was the FSD airframe that was forced to divert to Italy with a technical problem during its ferry flight from the USA to Israel on 10 December 1976. Despite this less than auspicious start to its career with the IDF/AF, Baz 646 ultimately became the only FSD jet to claim an aerial victory during its frontline career. Named *Raam* (Thunder) from 1981, the aircraft downed three MiG-21s and a MiG-23 between 31 December 1980 and 11 June 1982 – one of these successes was a rare cannon victory. With four SyAAF victory roundels on its nose, the aircraft is seen here on 24 October 2003 whilst being flown by 8.5-kill ace Moshe Melnik on his very last F-15 flight. A fully qualified Baz pilot for almost 27 years, Melnik accumulated 1500 flying hours in the F-15 during his long career. He claimed three kills with the Baz, and also introduced the system of naming individual aircraft in 1981**

**Left**
Baz 644 (F-15A 72-0118) was one of the three FSD airframes that arrived late in Israel on 10 December 1976 and triggered the collapse of the long-standing Israeli Labor government. Named *Barak* (Lightning) from 1981 onwards, the aircraft is seen here wearing a temporary paint scheme applied during trials in 1988. The latter were instigated by Double Tail Squadron CO Ram Caller, who was perhaps inspired by the Keith Ferris splinter schemes that he had encountered on several of the F-15s that he had flown with the 555th TFTS during his time at Luke AFB participating in the 1976 Term 2 F-15 conversion

Baz 622 (F-15A 72-0117) taxies out at the start of the first F-15 flight to be performed by an Israeli pilot in Israel on Sunday, 12 December 1976. Sat in the cockpit is Double Tail Squadron CO, Eitan Ben-Eliyahu. This aircraft was named *Saar* (Gale) in 1981, and following its retirement in the late 1990s, it has served as an instructional airframe at the IDF/AF Technical School in Haifa. The Baz FSD airframes were named after the first four jets to serve with the IDF/AF – Gloster Meteor T7s, which were delivered in 1953, and pioneered the Israeli tradition of allocating names to combat aircraft

Just 48 hours after the aircraft had arrived in Israel, Eitan Ben-Eliyahu taxied a Baz out of the unit's HAS and departed from Tel Nof's runway on the jet's first flight in IDF/AF service. He duly performed a stunning sequence of aerobatics over the airfield, although these were deemed to be a little 'too enthusiastic' for base commander Ran Ronen's liking! A short while later, Ronen and the IDF/AF's Chief Test Pilot Yitzhak 'Jeff' Peer became the first pilots to be checked out on the Baz in Israel.

As per standard IDF/AF procedure, a conversion course for each of the fighter types in frontline service commenced at the beginning of every term. The course usually lasted four months, and at the end of it pilots were assigned to their respective squadrons. New arrivals in the frontline were known as 'junior' pilots, and they were only declared operational in the air-to-ground mission at the end of their first Term with the squadron. If the squadron was a multi-role unit, then the new pilot was declared operational in the air-to-air mission at the end of his second Term. Senior pilots did not attend conversion courses, but were instead checked out in new types such as the F-15.

Just as the Baz was a huge leap forward for those that flew it in terms of its mission capabilities, the jet also changed the way groundcrews maintained aircraft in the frontline. Personnel working on the F-15 had to adjust to its integrated systems, rather than an electrician repairing malfunctions with the electronics, mechanics rectifying mechanical failures and weapon system specialists troubleshooting faulty mission computers and radars. With the Baz, a multi-disciplined approach was required by groundcrews when it came to fixing malfunctions.

In the early days of the F-15's service in Israel, the jet suffered from a series of wingtip structural failures, persistent fuel leaks and unreliability with the engine restarting system, although the aircraft's introduction to frontline use went smoothly overall. Indeed, most technical issues disappeared as maintenance crews grew more familiar with the jet.

Although occasionally temperamental on the ground, once in the air there was nothing to match the Baz, as Yoram Peled recalled;

'There were still only four jets in the squadron when we returned from the USA, although the delivery of new aircraft resumed shortly after we reached Tel Nof. Between 1977 and 1980 we ruled the skies over Israel,

flying a lot of air-to-air training missions as we trained the IDF/AF in how to fight next generation combat aircraft of the kind that was eventually expected to appear in the Middle East. The Sinai Peninsula was still our main training area then, and we routinely deployed there, flying all kinds of operational scenarios, including long-range escort missions.'

Although the initial IDF/AF operational requirement had been for 50 F-15s, only half this number was initially acquired due to the parlous state of the Israeli economy at the time and the political machinations of the US government. The aircraft was not only expensive to buy, but the Americans also viewed the incremental sale of F-15s to the IDF/AF as a way of preserving the fighter's power as a tool of diplomacy. And it was the latter factor more than anything else that dictated the timing of the second F-15 purchase. With a number of the 25 *Peace Fox* jets still to be delivered, Egypt and Israel launched a new round of negotiations that were made public when Egyptian President Anwar Sadat visited Israeli Prime Minister Menachem Begin in Jerusalem in November 1977.

To encourage Egypt, to reassure Israel and to strengthen support for the Egyptian-Israeli peace process among moderate Arab nations, the administration of US President Jimmy Carter announced a new arms package for the region on 14 February 1978. Egypt was to receive 50 F-5E fighters, Israel was promised 15 F-15s and 75 F-16s and Saudi Arabia was to be supplied with 60 F-15s. The US Congress approved the package on 16 May 1978. In the event, Egypt rejected the F-5Es in favour of ex-USAF F-4Es, but the remaining fighter types were supplied as promised. Egypt and Israel duly signed a peace treaty in March 1979.

The second batch of IDF/AF F-15s was valued at $283 million, and included nine F-15C single-seat jets and six F-15D two-seaters. These aircraft were improved versions of the F-15A/B, with increased internal fuel capacity, conformal fuel tank (CFT) compatibility, higher take-off weights and modernised avionics. While only eight per cent of the *Peace Fox* jets were two-seaters, 40 per cent of the *Peace Fox II* aircraft were F-15Ds. This higher than usual number of two-seat jets revealed that the IDF/AF had plans to utilise the Baz in long-range fighter operations, and to make them precision-guided munitions (PGM) capable in the future.

Deliveries of *Peace Fox II* F-15Ds finally commenced in August 1981, having been delayed by further diplomatic problems with the US government. By then the IDF/AF's F-15A/Bs had flown hundreds of operational sorties and claimed their first air-to-air kills.

## BAZ BAPTISM OF FIRE

The Palestinian Liberation Army (PLO), which had been founded by the Arab League in 1964 with the sole purpose of destroying the state of Israel, had suffered a major blow in its campaign when, in September 1970, King Hussein of Jordan expelled the group from his country. Determined to continue its armed struggle, the PLO turned Lebanon into its primary base from which to launch attacks on Israel.

Lebanon (like neighbouring Syria) had been under French Mandate from the end of World War One until it was granted independence in 1943. Syria had never relinquished its aspirations to annex Lebanon, and in an effort to seize power, it frequently tried to stir up trouble between Christian and Muslim factions in Lebanon.

Further unrest between these religious groups followed in the wake of the mass arrival of the PLO after its expulsion from Jordan. Following six years of fighting between Christians and Muslims, Syria intervened by occupying large areas of Lebanon in 1976. With Muslim factions now in the ascendancy in Lebanon, the PLO was encouraged to intensify its campaign of guerilla warfare against Israel.

On 11 March 1978, a group of 13 Palestinian Al Fatah terrorists sailed from Lebanon in Zodiac boats and came ashore on a beach near the Israeli town of Maagan Michael. They headed straight for the nearby coastal highway and hijacked a bus, which was pursued by an IDF unit led by future Prime Minister Ehud Barak. In the firefight which ensued near Herzliya, nine of the eleven terrorists aboard the bus were killed, as were 36 Israelis civilians. Dozens more were injured.

In the wake of the deadliest terrorist attack on Israel since its creation in 1948, the Begin government ordered the commencement of Operation *Litani* (named after the principal river in southern Lebanon) in an effort to destroy the PLO infrastructure in southern Lebanon.

IDF troops invaded Lebanon on 15 March 1978 and occupied the southern region of the country for six days. An Israeli-supported Lebanese Christian security zone was then established along the border with Israel, and this acted as a buffer zone between the latter country and PLO-controlled southern Lebanon.

Throughout Operation *Litani*, the Double Tail Squadron flew combat air patrols (CAPs) over southern Lebanon, defending both IDF troops on the ground and IDF/AF attack aircraft in the air. The Israeli press gave extensive coverage to the Baz's 'baptism of fire', claiming that the new IDF/AF jet acted as a 'flying radar station' over Lebanon.

Although Operation *Litani* had indeed given the Baz its operational debut, the jet had not been given the chance to prove its worth as a fighter in aerial combat for no Syrian or Lebanese aircraft have been sent aloft to dispute its mastery of the skies over southern Lebanon. Indeed, almost a year would pass before a major political upheaval in the modern history of the Middle East would trigger more intensive action over Lebanon. And this time the 'Baz's' capabilities as an interceptor would be put to the test.

The signing of the Israel-Egypt Peace Treaty in Washington, D.C. on 26 March 1979 rocked the Arab world. Libya clashed with Egypt, and succeeded in getting the latter country suspended from the Arab League for a decade, while Iraqi President Saddam Hussein began the build-up of a so-called 'Eastern Front' as a military replacement to the withdrawal of Egyptian forces in the war against Israel.

In reality, the 'Eastern Front' strategy, whereby the combined armies of Iraq, Jordan and Syria would engage Israel, was unrealistic in the short term due to military deficiencies in the Arab forces at that time. Syria, therefore, began to actively explore different options in an effort to keep up pressure on Israel. By maintaining the fight against the Zionists, Syria also cemented its place in the vanguard of those Arab nations that refused to accept the Egyptian peace initiative.

Just 16 days after the peace treaty had been signed, Syrian Air Force (SyAAF) fighter aircraft began overflights of Lebanon. Up until then, Israel had considered Lebanese skies to be a benign environment. The Lebanese Air Force was no match for the IDF/AF, and it had shown no interest in engaging Israeli jets, which regularly violated its airspace – IDF/AF reconnaissance aircraft routinely overflew Lebanon, collecting intelligence data that allowed attacks to be made on PLO targets.

The Israelis saw the SyAAF flights as a breach of the 'status quo', whilst the Syrians viewed them as an act of Arab solidarity. They also directly supported the activities of their ground forces, which had been in Lebanon since 1976. The significance of these flights to the wider Arab world should not be underestimated either, as Syrian Minister of Defence Mustafa Tlas plainly stated at the time;

'The decision to face the IDF/AF is an important one for us to take. The enemy has repeatedly taken advantage of its air superiority in order to launch attacks that have killed many Arabs in Lebanon and forced many others to flee the country. Can we stand by and allow the enemy such freedom of action? Should we ground our fighters and restrain our heroic pilots, who are so eager to engage the enemy despite the inevitable losses. Because these men are prepared to be victims for Syria in its ongoing struggle against Israel, the fighter pilots have continued to fly their missions.'

At first the IDF adopted a 'wait and see' policy as it evaluated the threat posed by the SyAAF. David Ivry, who was IDF/AF commander from 1977 to 1982, commented;

'Syrian flights over Lebanon were initially nothing more than a show of force, and as long as they did not threaten Israeli troops in southern Lebanon, we ignored them. Naturally, the IDF/AF was anxious to engage the Arab pilots, but we obeyed the guidelines issued to us by the Israeli government. Over time, the Syrians became more aggressive in their mission profiles, but our policy remained firm – we would not tolerate interference with our activities in the south of the country, but equally so, we would not go out of our way to target the Syrian aircraft either.'

However, two months after the first overflights, the SyAAF finally pushed the IDF/AF too far when the Arab pilots' growing self-confidence saw them attempt to intercept Israeli attack strike aircraft bombing PLO targets in southern Lebanon.

Relying on its extensive network of communication intelligence (COMINT) and signal intelligence (SIGINT) gathering sites along the Lebanese and Syrian borders, the Israelis were able to assemble an accurate order of battle for the SyAAF. They were also real-time monitoring the daily activities of the Syrian fighter units, which allowed them to second guess the mission profiles that the SyAAF was intending to fly over Lebanon.

Jets departing Syrian air bases were also quickly picked up by the chain of IDF/AF search radars, which operated without any real support from the Grumman E-2C Dayas (Kite) that had entered service in 1978, but had proven virtually useless when operating over land. The IDF/AF's monitoring efforts in the border region were further increased when Israeli combat aircraft were bombing PLO targets in Lebanon.

Strike aircraft were always allocated a fighter CAP whenever attacking targets, as per standard IDF/AF operational procedure. These CAPs were enhanced both in terms of the number of fighters committed and the type of aircraft employed in the wake of SyAAF overflights. In many ways, the protective CAP missions flown in the late spring and early summer of

1979 closely resembled the IDF/AF ambush tactics that was used to great effect during the War of Attrition.

An ambush attack was simple to perform, with the CAP consisting of three tiers of fighters – a protective CAP close to the attack aircraft's target, a back-up CAP further away and additional fighter formations on immediate alert at nearby IDF/AF bases. Those individuals manning the CAP jets were all hand picked, being the best fighter pilots in the IDF/AF. In 1979, they were usually proven MiG killers, with a handful also being aces. When an ambush was planned, it had top priority, which in turn meant that it was fully supported by GCU, radar-jamming and real-time COMINT and SIGINT assets.

However, the ambush was not a mission in itself, but a by-product of an air strike. If the SyAAF ignored the latter, then there would be no engagement, but if it reacted in an aggressive manner, the IDF/AF would call off the strike and ramp up the ambush. The various COMINT, SIGINT and radar operators monitoring Syrian airwaves and airspace were tasked with detecting any SyAAF response to the air strike.

Israeli jets bombed PLO targets in Lebanon on 24 April, 6, 8, 23 and 24 May, and 8 and 24 June 1979. There can be little doubt that the frequency of these strikes was increased in the wake of the Syrian overflights, as the IDF/AF attempted to lure the SyAAF into battle. And there was at least one close call prior to the Baz pilots finally getting an opportunity to demonstrate their fighter's superiority on 27 June 1979.

Tasked with defending an air strike aimed at PLO targets along the Lebanese Mediterranean coast between Sidon and Damur, the ambush team sortied by the Double Tail Squadron on that date was a formidable one. Leading the first line of defence was Benny Zinker, who had succeeded Eitan Ben-Eliyahu as Double Tail Squadron commander the previous month. Zinker's wingman was Flying School Fighter Training Squadron CO Moshe Melnik, who was also an Emergency Posting (EP) pilot assigned to the Double Tail Squadron. Ex-CO Ben-Eliyahu, who was also still flying with his old unit as an EP, was in the No 3 jet, and his wingman was Yoel Feldsho, who was the squadron's senior deputy CO.

The back-up CAP consisted of a mixed formation of Bazs and Kfirs, with the F-15s flown by Yoram Peled (the Double Tail Squadron's junior deputy commander) and Guy Golan. The Kfirs filled the Nos 3 and 4 slots in the formation.

The IDF/AF had first introduced mixed CAP formations during the War of Attrition, when two F-4s would routinely lead two Mirage IIICs. This decision had been made so that the superior radar in the lead jets would allow them to acquire the enemy aircraft, and thus vector the trailing aeroplanes into an interception. It also meant that all the fighter units in the IDF/AF got to participate in aerial combat, rather than just a select few pilots flying F-15s. Indeed, the solitary Baz squadron was the only unit to exclusively fly CAPs at this time, as all other fighter squadrons were tasked with flying strike and reconnaissance missions as well.

Therefore, in an effort to maintain a certain level of esprit de corps amongst all Israeli fighter pilots, and not just those flying F-15s, senior officers in the IDF/AF made sure that mixed CAPs were the order of the day during these limited-scale skirmishes over southern Lebanon in 1979-80. However, Kfir and F-4 pilots knew full well that should war

Eitan Ben-Eliyahu prepares to fly Baz 658 (F-15A 76-1506) *Typhoon* in July 1984 to mark the occasion of his final flight with the Double Tail Squadron, which he had commanded from 1976 to 1979. He had then been assigned to the unit as an EP until mid-1984. Ben-Eliyahu assumed command of Ramat David air base in August 1984, and he subsequently led the IDF/AF from 1996 until 2000

break out, the Double Tail Squadron would almost exclusively man the CAP slots due to the aircraft's unquestioned superiority in aerial combat.

At 1107 hrs on 27 June 1979, Israeli COMINT and SIGINT stations detected radio traffic indicating that Syrian radar had acquired IDF/AF attack aircraft flying along the Lebanese coastline. Three formations of SyAAF MiG-21s were scrambled to intercept the Israeli aircraft, but as they crossed the Lebanese-Syrian border, the IDF/AF jets withdrew west and the Arab interceptors were ordered by their fighter controllers to abort the mission and return to base.

At 1120 hrs Syrian radar operators detected more Israeli jets over Lebanon, so the SyAAF MiG-21s were again vectored to engage. One minute later, Israeli radio jamming blocked any communication between the Syrian pilots and personnel manning the Ground Control Intercept (GCI) stations. The latter then spotted F-15s popping up from low altitude on their radar screens, but they were unable to relay this information to the MiG-21 pilots due to radio jamming. The Baz pilots were now just moments away from their first clash with the SyAAF.

Flying the lead jets, Zinker and Melnik quickly achieved a radar lock on their targets and fired a single AIM-7F each in a BVR engagement. As was typical for this time of year, the weather was clear and sunny, allowing the Baz pilots to keep visual contact with the two large AAMs that they had just shot off. Time passed and the Sparrows disappeared from sight, having missed their targets. Both pilots could now see the MiG-21s, so Zinker and Melnik decided that it was time for WVR combat.

Spotting the two MiG-21s first, Melnik became the section leader and turned towards them, launching a Python 3 AAM as he closed on the enemy jets. Again, he kept his eyes glued on the missile's flightpath, and this time he was relieved to see it score a direct hit on the MiG-21, which duly broke apart into two large sections.

Although already a 5.5-kill ace F-4 ace, Melnik was so overwhelmed by this sight that he totally ignored the second SyAAF fighter. Fortunately, Yoel Feldsho was covering the lead section, and he fired an AIM-7F which destroyed the MiG-21 before if could get onto Melnik's tail.

The IDF/AF subsequently claimed that two four-ship formations of MiG-21s had been engaged on 27 June, with the back-up CAP intercepting the second quartet of SyAAF jets. Leading the mixed formation of F-15s and Kfirs was Yoram Peled, who recalled;

'We were on a low altitude CAP some 30 miles behind the high altitude CAP. Monitoring the radio calls between the latter jets and our GCU, I decided that if I maintained my present position, the battle would be over before we had caught up with the lead CAP. I was sure that if there was to be a clash between our fighters and the Syrian MiG-21s, it would last only a matter of minutes at most. Indeed, we were all convinced that the AIM-7Fs carried by our jets would shoot down the MiGs head-on in a BVR interception – these weapons missed their targets, of course, much to our disappointment. As the second line CAP, we could not use the BVR capability of our AIM-7Fs in any case due to the close proximity of friendly aircraft to enemy fighters.

'Ignoring the instructions given to us by our GCU, I closed the distance between my formation and the first line CAP as they in turn stalked the MiG-21s. By the time we were vectored to engage the second formation of enemy aircraft, we were pretty close to the lead CAP. Indeed, we were directly beneath them when they launched their AIM-7Fs. No one had been allocated specific targets by the GCU at this point in the interception, so once the lead CAP's AAMs missed, the MiG-21s broke formation and we entered the fray.

'Seeing two MiG-21s diving in a right-hand turn, I figured that I could shoot them down one after the other. I had started to point my

nose at them when I noticed a lone Baz engaging both jets. I did not know who the pilot of the F-15 was, but he was still outside their turn and I was in a better position just above them. I dropped my nose and launched an (AIM-9G) AAM that hit the trailing MiG-21 at the very moment that it was locked up in the gunsight of the chasing Baz. The pilot of the latter jet was momentarily surprised by the premature demise of his intended target, but he quickly recovered his composure and switched his attention to the MiG-21 lead. He destroyed the jet with a short burst of 20 mm cannon fire while I watched his back.

'When we landed, Eitan (Ben-Eliyahu) asked, "Who smashed that MiG right in front of my face?!" I reluctantly admitted that I had shot it down, and also apologised for taking the shot ahead of him – no true fighter pilot could have resisted such temptation, however. Fortunately, we were all so happy with the results of the mission that I was forgiven.'

During the WVR engagement, which had lasted just 60 seconds, the Double Tail Squadron had achieved four kills using all of the air-to-air weapons then available to the Baz – the AIM-7F, the AIM-9G, the Python 3 and the 20 mm cannon.

A fifth kill claimed during the course of the 27 June engagement was the subject of much debate between Baz pilot Guy Golan and his Kfir counterpart Shai Eshel. They had both launched AAMs at the same MiG-21, so they initially agreed to share the kill between them. However, the IDF/AF ultimately decided to award the kill to Eshel, as the Baz pilots had already been credited with four victories – an achievement without equal in IDF/AF jet fighter history.

The Gloster Meteor had been credited with two kills on its combat debut on 1 September 1955, while the Ouragan, Mystere, Super Mystere, Mirage IIIC and F-4E had only managed to claim a single victory apiece in their first air-to-air engagements. The F-15 was already living up to the IDF/AF's vision of it being a 'superfighter' that would

Yoel Feldsho lands Baz 704 at Tel Nof on 27 June 1979, having just downed a MiG-21 with an AIM-7F over southern Lebanon. As this photograph clearly reveals, he was alone in the F-15B when he claimed his kill. Indeed, it was not until 1981 that the Double Tail Squadron welcomed its first group of navigators. When Baz 704 claimed its second kill on 11 June 1982, the jet was fully crewed

Tel Nof air base CO Amos Amir (partially obscured in the very centre of this photo) greets the Baz pilots soon after they had returned from the 27 June 1979 clash. Immediately behind Amir is Moshe Melnik, while the others are (from the pilot to Amir's left, in a clockwise direction) Eran Blanche (obscured), Ronen Shapira, Guy Golan, Eitan Ben-Eliyahu (obscured), Yoram Peled, Dani Levit (back to camera), Benny Zinker (back to camera) and Yoel Feldsho (back to camera)

restore its much-vaunted claims-to-losses ratio from the Six Day War. However, the aircraft's ability to deter the enemy from challenging the IDF/AF, period, would take longer to achieve.

## DOUBLE SCORE

The introduction of the Baz had greatly increased the IDF/AF's air-to-air capabilities. Like the F-4E, the F-15 was armed with four IR AAMs, four SARH AAMs, a 20 mm cannon and a similar search radar system. However, the F-15 was a fourth generation fighter, which featured systems far in advance of those built into the veteran Phantom II. And for the first time in its history, the IDF/AF had a fighter that, in certain scenarios, provided its pilot with better radar coverage than the dedicated ground-based radar network.

The F-15's advanced capabilities, and the mission concepts created by the Double Tail Squadron to exploit them, soon filtered up from Tel Nof to IDF/AF staff officers through the assignments of Baz pilots to the command HQ. Eitan Ben-Eliyahu, for example, completed his tenure as squadron CO in May 1978 and was then assigned to the IDF/AF staff as Head of the Weapon Systems Department. Yoram Peled also became a staff officer following his frontline tour, heading up the Interception Section within the Operations Department.

Despite the one-sided engagement on 27 June 1979, the SyAAF continued to fly over Lebanon with increasing regularity. Israeli air strikes on PLO targets also increased in their intensity, and in response, the Syrians started to send MiG-23MS 'Flogger-Gs' on sweeps over Lebanon. And the swing-wing fighter soon made its presence felt when one almost downed an IDF/AF RF-4E reconnaissance aircraft with three AAMs, all of which exploded near to the wildly gyrating Phantom II.

This episode galvanised the IDF/AF in its efforts to achieve a level of deterrence over Lebanon for its reconnaissance and strike aircraft. An ambush attack was therefore planned for 24 September 1979, with Benny Zinker leading the two F-15s that formed the 'bait' section, and his senior deputy CO Avner Naveh heading up the main force four-ship formation. The Syrians duly scrambled a pair of MiG-21s to intercept Zinker and his wingman, followed by four more fighters to engage the main force.

Within 77 seconds of the engagement beginning, the Baz pilots had shot down four of the six MiG-21s sent aloft to intercept them. Naveh claimed the first kill with a Python 3, followed closely by Dedi Rosenthal, who downed his MiG with an AIM-7F, and Relik Shafir, who fired a single AIM-9G. Naveh then destroyed the fourth MiG-21 with a well-aimed burst of cannon fire.

Having become the first Baz pilot to achieve two kills, Naveh would add three more victories to his tally when next he engaged the SyAAF in combat. Shafir subsequently became the only Israeli pilot to be credited with kills in both the F-15 and F-16, while Rosenthal achieved fame as the IDF/AF Museum's Spitfire pilot – an aircraft he has flown since 1991.

## FIRST BAZ LOSS

Guy Golan returned to Israel from routine F-15 simulator training in the USA on Wednesday, 24 September 1979, which was the very day that his fellow Baz pilots doubled their kill tally.

**These photographs, taken on 24 September 1979 by the HUD camera fitted to Baz 695, show the first of two MiG-21s destroyed by Avner Naveh on this date. This SyAAF aircraft was downed by a Python 3 AAM – note that the F-15 was in a 6.2G turn when these photographs were taken. Moments later, Naveh gunned down his second MiG-21 with a deadly burst from his jet's M61A1 Vulcan 20 mm cannon**

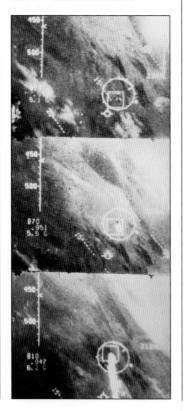

On 24 September 1979, Baz 692 (F-15A 76-1520) was used by Relik Shafir to claim his one and only Baz kill. Within a year Shafir had joined the IDF/AF F-16 Set-Up Team, and he duly became the only Israeli pilot to be credited with kills in both the F-15 and the F-16. Baz 692 did not enjoy Shafir's good fortune, however, as his MiG-21 kill remains the jet's sole victory to date – hence the solitary SyAAF symbol below its cockpit. The fighter was named *Galaxy* in 1981

Baz 676 also emerged victorious from the 24 September 1979 clash with the SyAAF over southern Lebanon, Dedi Rosenthal claiming a MiG-21 with a single AIM-7F. Five days later, the jet became the IDF/AF's first F-15 casualty when it stalled and crashed during a bad weather landing at night at Tel Nof. Pilot Guy Golan, who had been a junior member of the second Baz conversion course of Year 1976 Term 3, perished in the accident. Golan had accumulated 347 flying hours in F-15s prior to his death

Golan had graduated from Flying School Class 71 on 12 July 1973 as one of the four top students in his class. He then attended the A-4 OTU during IDF/AF Year 1973 Term 3 and flew the Skyhawk and the Phantom II, prior to undertaking his F-15 conversion in America. The inclusion of Golan amongst the first ten Israeli pilots to transition onto the Baz gives an indication of his abilities in the cockpit. These ten individuals were indeed the best fighter pilots in the IDF/AF at the time, and great things were expected of them. Most fulfilled their promise.

Eitan Ben-Eliyahu led the IDF/AF from 1996 until 2000, while Moshe Melnik, Avner Naveh, Yoel Feldsho and Benny Zinker retired as brigadier generals. Alex Gan ended his career as a colonel, while Ram Caller was killed in a mid-air collision whilst flying a Baz, having attained the rank of lieutenant colonel and been given command of the Double Tail Squadron. F-15 ace Yoram Peled retired as a lieutenant colonel after commanding the First Fighter Squadron from 1984 until 1989 – the same unit that his father Beni Peled had led twice during the 1950s.

Peled knew Guy Golan well, stating that 'he was a special pilot, with great intelligence. I believe that had he still been alive today, he would have been commander of the IDF/AF. Golan was made of the right stuff'.

On the night of 28/29 September 1979, Guy Golan was manning the readiness jet at Tel Nof. It was the first evening of the weekend, and all was quiet, with the base being seemingly deserted aside from Golan and his groundcrew. Yoram Peled, who had returned from the USA with Golan four days earlier, kept him company at the readiness HAS.

Soon after midnight, Yoram Peled, who was not on duty, decided to ride his motorcycle to his parents' house, where Beni Peled and his wife were watching over the F-15 pilot's children. As Peled rode away from the

HAS, he was enveloped in thick fog, so he quickly returned to the HAS and told Golan that he could go to sleep, as he figured that no pilot would be asked to fly on such a foggy night.

However, at 0230 hrs on 29 September 1979, Golan was indeed scrambled on what proved to be a futile, and ultimately bogus, interception. Returning to land at Tel

Nof after just 20 minutes aloft, he entered the circuit to land, but during his descent from the downwind to base leg Golan's jet stalled and crashed – the pilot was killed on impact. A close examination of the wreckage over the coming weeks revealed no evidence to suggest a technical malfunction. There was obviously nothing wrong with Baz 676, which had been credited with an air-to-air kill just days prior to the crash.

There was speculation at Tel Nof that Golan should not have been scrambled, or that he should have flown an instruments approach to the runway. Others stated that the sink rate of the still relatively heavy Baz returning to base after only a short flight was much higher than usual, and the pilot did not realise this in the poor weather. Ultimately, the IDF/AF Accident Investigation Board stated that the cause of the crash was 'personnel – aircrew', which was official terminology for pilot error.

## MORE COMBAT

The IDF/AF halted its air strikes on PLO targets in Lebanon in October 1979, and no such attacks were conducted for almost a year. Without any Israeli aircraft to challenge, the SyAAF also scaled back its overflights. By then the Baz had already established a degree of air superiority over Lebanon that had seen the Syrians suffer a kills-to-losses ratio of 9-to-0 in favour of the Israelis – F-15 pilots had accounted for eight of these kills.

Yet despite these statistics, the IDF/AF was finding it difficult to deter the SyAAF from challenging it over Lebanon. Syrian pilots were fully aware of the extent of the coverage of the Israeli command & control network, as well as the absolute superiority of the F-15 over the MiG-21. Even the introduction of the MiG-23 and MiG-25 into SyAAF service had little impact on the aerial balance of power, for they were only available in small numbers, and were inferior to the F-15 in any case. Indeed, there was nothing that the Soviet Union could offer the Syrian leadership that would counter-balance the F-15's superiority. The technological leap forward that the Americans had achieved with the Eagle effectively marked the beginning of the US victory in the Cold War.

Yet brave Syrian fighter pilots continued to challenge IDF/AF operations over Lebanon whenever they were ordered to do so, thus proving that the Baz had not yet delivered total deterrence in the region.

Air strikes against PLO targets resumed in August 1980 following a series of botched attempts by the terrorist group to attack Israel from the air. The first of these was frustrated by a technical malfunction on 20 July 1980 when the hot air balloon the PLO was planning on using to get across the border exploded during inflation.

In response, the IDF launched Operation *Movil* (Leader) on the night of 18/19 August, which saw a large-scale heliborne assault made against four PLO bases in southern Lebanon. As the Israeli troops pulled out of these areas, the IDF/AF launched air strikes on the morning of the 19th to cover their extraction by helicopter. More targets were bombed the following day, and the Palestinians claimed that *Movil* had been timed to coincide with a visit to the area by PLO leader Yasser Arafat.

On the afternoon of 24 August, the SyAAF scrambled four MiG-21s in an effort to intercept two IDF/AF RF-4Es conducting a reconnaissance mission over southern Lebanon. At 1645 hrs local time, the Phantom IIs' frontline CAP (two F-15s leading two Kfirs) was vectored into position to

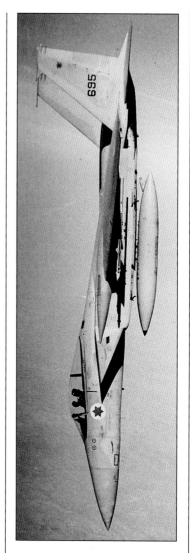

Baz 695 (F-15A 76-1521) was named *Ha Kochav* (The Star) in 1981, undoubtedly because it was then the top scoring Baz in IDF/AF service with 2.5 kills. All of these victories were historically significant, as the first two, claimed by Avner Naveh on 24 September 1979, made the jet the first double MiG killer, while Yoav Stern's MiG-21 on 31 December 1980 was the first shared victory credited to the F-15. Oran Hampel added another MiG-21 to Baz 695's tally on 9 June 1982. Adorned with two kill markings, which date this photograph as having been taken between late September 1979 and late December 1980, Baz 695 is looped during a training sortie over Israel

engage the Syrian jets. The Baz section leader targeted the leading two MiG-21s and his wingman engaged the second pair of Arab fighters.

The first two Syrian jets turned away as soon as they realised that they were being targeted by the F-15, but the pair allocated to wingman Ilan Margalit (in Baz 696) continued towards him. They were still on a collision course when Margalit fired an AIM-7F at the lead MiG-21. He followed the missile until it struck its target and caused the jet to explode – the Israeli pilot saw the disintegrating fighter spin down into a bank of cloud below him. Although Margalit had not seen the pilot eject from the stricken MiG-21, Nabil Girgis had indeed escaped from his aircraft, and he subsequently landed near a Lebanese village. He was duly handed over to Syrian forces in Lebanon by the local residents.

Following this clash, the SyAAF claimed that its jets had attempted to intercept IDF/AF combat aircraft that were bombing PLO targets in Lebanon. However, the Israelis stated that they were carrying out a reconnaissance mission at the time, but denied that there were any air strikes taking place in the area when the clash occurred. The following day, the four MiG-21 pilots involved in the action were interviewed on Syrian television, and one of them stated that 'Our orders are to be on readiness to engage Israeli flights over Lebanon. The Palestinians and Syrians are fighting the same war, and the Palestinian organisations in Lebanon are an integral part of the Syrian Army'.

Israeli jets again bombed PLO targets in Lebanon on 22 October 1980 when an air strike struck the town of En-Dorfil, which was located just 16 kilometres from the suburbs of south Beirut. The Israeli government stated that the strike was part of the ongoing fight against the PLO. Despite the attack taking place well north of the hotly contested southern border, the strike aircraft were not engaged by SyAAF fighters.

PLO targets in southern Lebanon were hit once more on 7 November 1980, although again the SyAAF stayed firmly on the ground. Following this mission, the Israeli government came to the conclusion that IDF/AF activity in southern Lebanon would not provoke an aerial response from the Syrians. In turn, it instructed the IDF to adopt the 'red line' policy,

Ilan Margalit was flying Baz 696 (F-15A 76-0522) when he was credited with a MiG-21 kill on 24 August 1980. This proved to be Margalit's sole victory, and Baz 696 has not scored since either. Named *Haziz* (Firecracker) from 1981, the aircraft is here in December 1978 during one of the first DACT deployments made by the Double Tail Squadron to Etszion air base

whereby the IDF/AF accepted SyAAF overflights over most of Lebanon and did not send its aircraft against targets beyond a certain latitude. Syria, in turn, avoided intercepting Israeli aircraft conducting missions over southern Lebanon. However, in reality, neither the Israelis nor the Syrians paid much attention to the aerial buffer zone created by the 'red line', with IDF/AF strike aircraft regularly hitting PLO targets all the way up to Beirut, and the SyAAF flying over southern Lebanon.

On 31 December 1980, the IDF/AF again hit PLO strongholds in southern Lebanon, but this time the Syrians scrambled a four-ship formation of MiG-21s to intercept the Israeli jets. The SyAAF aircraft were opposed by a mixed formation of two F-15s leading two F-4Es. Wingman Yair Rachmilevic, in Baz 646, shot down a MiG-21 with a Python 3 AAM to give the F-15 its tenth aerial victory, but just who destroyed the second aircraft was harder to prove.

The Phantom II section leader had been in position to fire his AAM when the F-4 suffered a weapon system malfunction, so the wingman shot off two missiles instead, but both of these failed to guide. He then launched a third AAM just as F-15 formation leader Yoav Stern, in Baz 695, also fired an AIM-9G. This time the missiles found their mark, and the kill was subsequently split between them.

Both pilots ejected over southern Lebanon, and contemporary reports at the time indicated that local villagers killed one of them after they mistook him for an Israeli aviator. IDF sources, however, figured that the Lebanese knew full well that the pilot was from the SyAAF, and that they were merely expressing their true anti-Syrian feelings.

## FIRST MiG-25 KILL

Despite these losses, the Syrians refused to allow the IDF/AF to operate over southern Lebanon totally unopposed. MiG-21 and MiG-23 pilots knew that their mounts were totally outclassed by Israeli F-15s, yet they remained committed to combat with the IDF/AF.

Desperately seeking some kind of aerial victory, the SyAAF focused its efforts on operational scenario in which its pilots had some hope of inflicting damage on the IDF/AF – the destruction of an RF-4E over Lebanon. Although the latter appeared to be easy prey, lacking any form of defensive armament, these aircraft were high value assets that never ventured outside Israeli airspace without a multi-layered CAP in close attendance. The RF-4E's flightpath was also closely monitored by the IDF/AF's all-seeing ground-based radar system.

The Israelis successfully frustrated Syrian attempts to intercept the reconnaissance aircraft with their MiG-21s, as the latter could not climb fast enough to attack the high-flying RF-4Es with their WVR AAMs – the SyAAF fighters lacked BVR capability. Even the MiG-23 struggled to catch the Phantom II, although the 'Flogger-G's' ability to fire BVR AAMs made it a more deadly foe.

The best aircraft that the USSR could supply to the SyAAF for this type of mission was the MiG-25P 'Foxbat-E' interceptor, and Syria became the first export customer for the world's fastest interceptor in late 1979. Once Arab pilots had achieved initial operational capability with the MiG-25, they were immediately tasked with putting an end to RF-4E overflights of Lebanon.

The close monitoring of Syrian airspace by IDF/AF COMINT and SIGINT stations had revealed the introduction of the MiG-25 into frontline service in late 1980, and from the following month onwards, these same sources detected several SyAAF attempts to intercept RF-4Es with the 'Foxbat-E'. As usual, the Israelis responded to this new threat by ordering an ambush mission to be flown.

Double Tail Squadron commander Benny Zinker was chosen to fly Baz 672 as the leader of the CAP charged with protecting an RF-4C on 13 February 1981. The weather was very poor, and the Israeli pilots were sceptical that the SyAAF would attempt an interception in such conditions. BVR missiles work just as well in poor weather, however, and soon the IDF/AF's radar network had acquired a target. David Ivry, who was IDF/AF commander from 1977 to 1982, recalled;

'The Syrian fighter was flying an interception course, accelerating very fast. The distances between the radar blips were such that it was obvious that the fighter was either a MiG-23 or a MiG-25.'

The Baz pilots were flying over the Sea of Galilee when they were notified that a Syrian interceptor had been scrambled. Although climbing through 30,000 ft, and still some 70 miles away from the leading Baz, the MiG was locked up by the radar in Zinker's jet. A vector to engage soon followed from the GCU tracking the SyAAF fighter, and the order was also given for the RF-4E crew to abort its reconnaissance mission. By now the leading pair of Baz fighters was over the town of Kiryat Shmona, and just short of the Israeli-Lebanese border. Zinker zoom-climbed to 50,000 ft, but then descended in order to remain below the Syrian jet.

Sticking to his preflight brief, Zinker launched his first AIM-7F at a range of 25 miles and his second immediately afterwards, by which point the jets were within 21 miles of each other. Zinker then hesitated momentarily, before launching a third Sparrow on his own initiative in order to make sure of his kill. Moments later there was a huge explosion, and Zinker noticed a lot of debris, although it was impossible for him to identify exactly what type of Syrian interceptor he had destroyed from such a distance. By now the Israeli pilot was flying over Syrian territory, so he quickly turned west and headed in the direction of the second Baz pair that had taken off with him. The kill was definite, but the identity of the Syrian interceptor was still unknown.

A Soviet delegation was sent out to Syria to debrief the SyAAF soon after the 13 February 1981 clash, and almost two weeks after the combat

The pilot of Baz 672 looks over at the camera whilst taxiing past Fouga Magister trainers in early 1972. Yoram Peled claimed a MiG-21 kill with this jet on 27 June 1979, and Benny Zinker was credited with the IDF/AF's first victory over the MiG-25 whilst flying it on 13 February 1981. Named *Tornado* that same year, the aircraft was lost in a collision with Baz 684 on 15 August 1988 while being flown by Ehud Falk – both Falk and the pilot of the other F-15, squadron CO Ram Caller, were killed. The jets had collided during an Air Combat Manoeuvring Instrumentation (ACMI) range training session. Although this advanced system could actually predict that the F-15s were going to hit each other well before they collided, the operating programme for the ACMI did not include a flight safety warning function at that time. Fellow F-15 reserve pilots who devised the BVR syllabus for the ACMI range prior to the accident, and who then developed an autonomous warning system in the wake of the collision, named their programme Ehud in memory of Falk

had taken place, it was reported that the jet shot down over Lebanon had indeed been a MiG-25P.

## HIGH-LOW MIX

As previously mentioned in this chapter, the 1978 arms deal signed between the US government and the Israelis covered the supply of 15 F-15C/Ds as part of *Peace Fox II* and 75 F-16A/Bs in a project codenamed *Peace Marble*. Just as the IDF/AF had selected the F-15 over the F-14, so the USAF had opted for the F-16 rather than the YF-17, which was later developed into the US Navy's F/A-18. By making this choice, the IDF/AF had followed the USAF model of a mixed fighter fleet that consisted of larger and more expensive F-15s bolstered by cheaper, and smaller, F-16s.

Although the F-16A lacked the BVR engagement capability of the F-15, it was nevertheless a fourth generation jet that was even more deadly in a WVR fight than the Eagle.

Examples of the F-16A/B Netz (Sparrowhawk) started arriving in Israel in July 1980, and when the first squadrons achieved initial operational capability with the aircraft, the Baz lost its air-to-air monopoly over Lebanon. The F-15 was indeed unbeatable in the air at this time, but the IDF/AF was keen to see as many of its units exposed to aerial combat over Lebanon as possible.

In early 1980 the Israelis could only field a single squadron of fourth generation jet fighters, but by the end of 1981 this number had risen to four. The IDF/AF knew that it had to introduce the F-16 into service as quickly as possible so that it could maintain air superiority over Lebanon, and therefore deter the SyAAF from further incursions over IDF-controlled territory. As a result of the high-low fighter model, the Baz was credited with just two aerial victories in 1981, while pilots flying newly-arrived F-16s claimed three kills.

The first two victories scored by the latter jet were directly responsible for a major escalation in the conflict in Lebanon. Two F-16s shot down a pair of Syrian Mil Mi-8 helicopters that were supporting a Syrian offensive against Christian militiamen in Zahle, in the Lebanon Valley. And although the SyAAF was prepared to lose a handful of fighters in sporadic aerial engagements with the IDF/AF, direct Israeli intervention against helicopters supporting troops some distance from southern Lebanon was a violation of the 'red line' policy according to the Syrians.

With their fighters outclassed by the IDF/AF's F-15s and F-16s, the only viable option open to the Syrians was to protect their ground forces through the movement of ADF units into the Lebanon Valley. By May 1981 the Syrians had an IADS up and running, and this greatly restricted the IDF/AF's freedom of movement over Lebanon.

In an effort to regain the initiative, the IDF/AF planned a suppression of enemy air defences (SEAD) offensive against Syrian IADS sites in the Lebanon Valley. The Israeli government refused to sanction such an operation, however, for its efforts were focused elsewhere on a mission that it deemed to be crucial in securing stability in the Middle East. The insertion of Syrian IADS into Lebanon was certainly a nuisance, but its neutralisation was secondary in importance to an operation that been planned and then rehearsed since late 1980. Following months of preparation, the Israeli government was on the verge of authorising the IDF/AF to launch Operation *Opera*, whose aim it was to destroy Iraq's sole nuclear reactor.

## OSIRAK RAID

Egypt's historical decision to negotiate peace with Israel in the late 1970s had left the Arab world in disarray. Many Muslim countries would follow the Egyptian lead in coming years, but the process of recognition of the Jewish state was a slow and painful one. Indeed, several fundamentalist regimes aspired to take over Egypt's position as leader of the Arab world by adopting a militant stance against Israel.

Syria clashed with Israel over Lebanon, for example, while Iraq, which shared no border with Israel, opted to develop nuclear weapons in an effort to rival Jewish military might in the region following its acquisition of an Osiris class research reactor from France. Construction began on the reactor (dubbed Osirak by the French) at the Al Tuwaitha Nuclear Centre site, south of Baghdad, in 1979.

Israeli Intelligence reported that Iraq's primary objective for Osirak was the production of a nuclear bomb. Following the receipt of this information the Israeli government launched a two-pronged effort to deny Iraq the option of employing nuclear weapons. The diplomatic path achieved nothing, however, for in the wake of the Iranian revolution in 1979, the West (and the USA in particular) viewed Iraq as an enlightened counterbalance to Ayatollah Khomeini and his regime. It was therefore unwilling to confront Iraq over its development of nuclear weapons.

Having failed on the diplomatic front, the Israeli government began to evaluate a military solution to the neutralisation of Osirak as a threat. The key to such an operation was the long-range strike capability that only the IDF/AF could provide.

The first planning iteration for such a mission was an assault modelled on the July 1976 operation that freed Israeli hostages in Entebbe, Uganda. The insertion of troops was quickly dropped in favour of an air raid, although when this mission was first mooted in 1979, the IDF/AF was simply unable to conduct such a long-range strike operation.

At that time, Israeli in-flight refuelling assets consisted of a handful of KC-130 tankers and a few A-4s fitted with buddy refueling stores. The principal bomber then in frontline service was the F-4E, which was capable of expending precision-guided munitions (PGM), but could not fly the required mission profile without in-flight refuelling – and the latter was deemed to be too dangerous to conduct in Iraqi skies.

As noted in Chapter 1, the Baz had been purchased after Israel Baharav had explained the jet's long-range attack potential to the Minister of Defence. However, Baharav's presentation was based on the assumption that the F-15's Fuel And Sensor Tactical (FAST) pack would be developed into a combat capable system. Baharav's vision was fully justified when Conformal Fuel Tanks (CFTs) were supplied as part of the F-15C/D contract signed in 1979. However, no CFTs were available to Israel at the time of the initial planning for the Osirak raid, and the Baz then lacked the PGM competence of the F-4E in any case.

Although the Iranian Revolution had spelled the end of Israel's diplomatic drive to deny Iraq nuclear weapons, it proved to be a blessing for those championing the military option. Iran had been scheduled to receive its F-16s before Israel, but with the overthrowing of the Shah, production slots for these jets were given to the IDF/AF instead.

The rescheduled F-16 delivery dates were crucial to the eventual success of the Osirak raid, since they meant that jets would now enter IDF/AF service prior to the 'point of no return'. The latter was defined as the day that the Osirak plant was activated, after which it could not be bombed for fear of releasing radioactive matter into the atmosphere. Israeli Intelligence reports indicated that Osirak would be declared 'hot' by the Iraqis sometime in 1981.

Soon after the first F-16s started to arrive in Israel in July 1980, senior pilots flying the Netz began to evaluate long-range profile options with the jet. Thanks to its advanced bombing computer, the aircraft would be able to hit the reactor with conventional Mk 84 2000-lb general purpose (GP) 'iron' bombs, rather than having to use PGMs, which were deemed to be too small to knock out Osirak in any case. The F-16 would be at the very limit of its unrefuelled operational radius of action when carrying two Mk 84s and three tanks, however.

At about this time McDonnell Douglas supplied Israel with the first of nine CFT packs for its F-15s. With these fitted, the Baz could fly to Osirak and deliver two GP bombs apiece almost as accurately as the F-16 and still have plenty of fuel to make it home. Tel Nof base CO Avihu Ben Nun duly explained to IDF/AF commander David Ivry that bombed-up F-15s fitted with CFTs would be the best option for the attack on Osirak. Ivry rejected this suggestion, however, stating that the Netz pilots handpicked for the strike had already mastered the long-range mission profile. He also pointed out that there were only nine CFT packs available, which meant that a force of just four jets could be sortied.

In September 1980 Iraq attacked Iran to start the first Gulf War, and soon after the conflict commenced, F-4Es from the Islamic Republic of Iran Air Force bombed the Osirak site. This was bad news for the Israelis, as the IDF/AF knew that during wartime, the defences protecting such a high value target as Osirak would be bolstered and the Iraqi ADF would maintain a high state of alert. As a direct result of this attack, the F-15 was back in the fight, as CFT-equipped jets would be responsible for defending the bombers all the way to Baghdad and back.

Double Tail Squadron commander Benny Zinker was to lead the Baz force on the Osirak raid, which was scheduled for 10 May 1981. He selected Flying School Fighter Stream commander and Baz EP pilot Moshe Melnik as his wingman. The force was assembled, armed, briefed and ready to go on the 10th as planned when the operation was abruptly called off. The raid was then rescheduled to 7 June. By then Melnik had become Double Tail Squadron CO, and he assumed the role of F-15 force lead, with Zinker now acting as his wingman.

Melnik chose to fly an F-15B on this mission, with fellow Baz pilot Yair Rachmilevic occupying the backseat of the leading jet. Both fighters trailed the F-16s on the mission, with the F-15s configured for air combat through the fitment of four AIM-7Fs and four AIM-9Gs. They also carried electronic warfare (EW) pods. Included in the second pair of Baz fighters was another F-15B, flown by Mickey Lev. This aircraft was equipped with improvised high frequency (HF) radio communications equipment, including a long antenna glued to the outside of the Baz's large canopy.

The HF operator in the backseat of the Baz was none other than the commander of the IDF/AF's Operations Department, Aviem Sella, who had headed up the Osirak raid planning team, and who was now acting as an airborne communication relay between the attacking jets and the command & control centre in Israel. Sella was one of three full colonels participating in the mission, with Ramat David air base commander Yiftach Spector flying as wingman to the leader of the second F-16 four-ship formation, and Weapon Systems Department CO Eitan Ben-Eliyahu heading up the second F-15 formation, with Yoram Peled as his wingman.

Except for Ben-Eliyahu, who almost had to abort the mission due to a fuel system malfunction in his jet, the F-15s' participation in the Osirak raid was absolutely eventless. If Iraqi interceptors had attempted to attack the F-16s, the latter were relying exclusively on the Bazs to ensure their safe return home. As it was, not a single enemy aircraft attempted to engage the jets on their 1200-mile round trip from Israel. One of the F-15 pilots who participated in the mission later recalled;

'The F-16s bombed the target and we did nothing, but we were there nonetheless – three pairs of F-15s. Our fuel state was not much better than the strike aircraft, as we also flew the ingress to the target at low altitude. Granted, we had CFTs fitted to our jets, but we also had two engines. Had enemy aircraft made an appearance, it would have been a complicated engagement fought a long way from home, but we would have prevailed.'

## SECOND MiG-25 KILL

Whilst the Israeli government dealt with the criticism that came its way from around the globe following the Osirak strike, the IDF/AF returned to bombing targets closer to home in southern Lebanon. July saw a dramatic increase in the number of sorties being flown, with multiple strike missions taking place on a daily basis from the 10th through to the 23rd. The PLO responded by using artillery pieces that it had hidden throughout southern Lebanon to shell Israel.

The only attempt made by the SyAAF to intercept an attack mission came on 14 July, and it ended with the destruction of a MiG-21 by an F-16. US mediation then yielded a ceasefire between Israel and the PLO that lasted almost a year.

In line with the agreement, the IDF/AF refrained from flying attack missions over southern Lebanon during this period. However, reconnaissance overflights continued unabated, and on 29 July 1981, having failed to defend the PLO for much of the renewed fighting, the SyAAF tried to restore some pride by intercepting an RF-4E.

The Syrians vectored two MiG-21s and a pair of MiG-25s onto a

Shaul Simon was flying Baz 673 *Ha Oketz* (The Sting) when he was credited with the F-15's second MiG-25 kill on 29 July 1981. This photograph shows the jet landing at Tel Nof, having just completed an air-to-ground training mission – note the empty SUU-20 training bomb dispenser on the centreline fuselage pylon. Emphasising the F-15's multi-role capabilities, the aircraft has empty AIM-9 dual launcher rails above each of the external fuel tanks. Although Israel purchased the F-15 primarily to achieve air superiority in the Middle East, most early Baz pilots had previously flown F-4Es, and were therefore more accustomed to a multi-role platform that was perhaps more of a strike aircraft than a fighter. Moreover, with the IDF/AF being a proponent of mission flexibility when it came to the employment of its fast jet types, even the Baz was occasionally treated as a 'mud mover'. And it was his pilots' proficiency in the latter mission that motivated Tel Nof air base commander Avihu Ben-Nun to propose that the F-15 'bomber' exclusively undertake the Osirak strike on 7 June 1981

Phantom II nearing the end of its mission over southern Lebanon, and Double Tail Squadron reserve pilot Shaul Simon (in Baz 673) responded to their move with a single AIM-7F, fired WVR. The missile chased down its target in a matter of seconds, destroying a 'Foxbat-E'.

The MiG formations had split up just prior to the Sparrow reaching its target, so the two F-15s were vectored onto the pair of MiG-21s that were fleeing eastwards in the direction of the Syrian border. Unable to get within missile-firing distance, the F-15 pilots gave up the chase and turned towards Israel.

The pilot of the sole surviving MiG-25, who had been waiting patiently for the Bazs to break off their pursuit, launched two BVR AAMs at the F-15s moments after they had pointed their noses south. Evading the missiles, the Israeli pilots then attempted to chase down the second 'Foxbat-E', but the big fighter easily accelerated away from them.

## DACT

Until 1980, and the arrival of the F-16, the Baz had been the IDF/AF's sole fourth generation fighter, allowing its pilots to enjoy total superiority over any other Israeli fast jet type – F-4E, Kfir, Nesher, Mirage IIIC and A-4. Because of its equipment, the Double Tail Squadron was tasked with training all IDF/AF fighter pilots in the tactics they needed to employ in order to evade fourth generation combat aircraft. However, the F-15 was so much better than the five types previously listed that tactics alone provided the pilots of these jets with little defence in an unrestricted DACT engagement.

For example, in a February 1977 training session, a seasoned Mirage IIIC ace was alarmed to learn that his less experienced opponent strapped into the cockpit of a Baz needed only 20 seconds to shake the Dassault jet off his tail and achieve an identical firing position. And this was against an aircraft type that up until then had been the IDF/AF's best WVR air combat platform.

In an effort to offset the F-15's superiority, most DACT sessions usually saw the Baz outnumbered by its opponents – typically, two 'superior' jets would engage three 'inferior' fighters. Yet even then the F-15s usually emerged as the winners, having simulated the shooting down of all three opponents within two to three minutes.

These 'superior' versus 'inferior' DACT sessions were also important for the F-15 pilots, who had to be prepared to engage previous generation SyAAF fighters for real over Lebanon.

Working their way through a dedicated DACT syllabus, codenamed Panther, Double Tail Squadron aircrews would deploy to Etszion air base, in Sinai, from Tel Nof for their training. In 1981, all adversary training was shifted to Ovda air base, and Panther courses continue to be run from here to this day. As part of the syllabus, F-15 pilots would fly against Kfirs simulating the MiG-21 and MiG-23.

For a fighter pilot, conducting a DACT mission against a Baz was almost as exciting as seeing real action against the SyAAF, for every Israeli fast jet pilot wanted to return to his squadron debriefing room with gun camera film or a HUD VTR cassette capturing an F-15 kill.

DACT hops between the Baz and previous generation fighters were the most hazardous peacetime missions flown by the IDF/AF, and it was because of this fact that regular F-15 versus F-16 sorties were officially barred during the first four years of the latter jet's service in Israel.

Double Tail Squadron aircrew viewed their contemporaries in the Netz units as frustrated Baz pilots who had failed to make it into the IDF/AF's leading fighter outfit. As a result of this 'war of words', F-16 pilots were eager to prove that the nimble Netz was more than a match for the much bigger Baz. Senior officers in the IDF/AF were fully aware of this simmering rivalry, and they concluded that DACT conducted between the two types as part of the units' normal day-to-day training regime could easily result in the loss of men and machines.

Only one exception to the no DACT rule was allowed during the early stages of the Netz's IDF/AF career when six Bazs secretly deployed to Ramat David air base soon after the F-16's arrival in Israel. A handful of the very best F-15 pilots subsequently flew six 1-v-1 sorties and a single 2-v-2 mission against the Netz, with these flights being structured in such a way that the WVR capabilities of both aircraft could be directly compared. Yoram Peled, who was by then a Flying School squadron commander and a Double Tail Squadron EP, flew one of the 1-v-1 sorties. He subsequently recalled;

'I flew against Amir Nachumi in an F-16B, and he had Yiftach Spector in the backseat – these men were both high-scoring aces, and we had all previously flown in the same F-4 squadron together. If my memory serves me right, our pair won the 2-v-2 training session, but in a 1-v-1 scenario, the Baz was no match for the Netz. The latter jet has to be the world's best WVR fighter platform.'

## TWO SQUADRONS

Five years after its activation, the Double Tail Squadron was a combat-proven outfit with two MiG-25 and 10.5 MiG-21 kills to its credit. Soviet fourth generation fighters were still years away from service entry, and in the Middle East no aircraft would be in a position to challenge the Baz for almost a decade.

Although the unit had lost a single jet in an accident, additional improved *Peace Fox II* F-15C/Ds had been delivered to the squadron

Baz 950 *Kherev Pipyot* (Sharp Sword) was the first of six F-15Ds delivered to Israel from 25 August 1981 as part of *Peace Fox II*. The jet is seen here in Spearhead Squadron markings soon after the unit was established on 16 June 1982. This aircraft would later be marked up with the squadron's distinctive red wedges on the inboard surfaces of its vertical stabilisers, these being applied in 1991 so that Sharp Sword jets could be easily differentiated from Double Tail Squadron aircraft. The latter unit had had its jets marked with an Eagle Head atop the inboard surfaces of their vertical stabilisers since 1982

from August 1981. These new aircraft further improved the unit's mission capabilities, and the arrival of nine CFT sets at around this time had allowed the IDF/AF to conduct long-range operations into Iraq.

By early 1982, the Double Tail Squadron was almost twice the size of a normal IDF/AF fighter unit, although there were still not enough F-15s in frontline service at any one time to justify the activation of a second squadron. However, renewed US diplomatic efforts in the Middle East again benefited the Israeli F-15 force in the wake of an arms deal struck between the administration of newly-elected President Ronald Reagan and Saudi Arabia.

In early 1981, the US government agreed to supply the Saudis with Boeing E-3 AWACS aircraft and to upgrade their F-15s to enable them to conduct air-to-ground missions. In an effort to deflect Israeli objections to this deal, the Americans also proposed to supply the IDF/AF with additional F-15C/Ds. By April 1982 the US proposal had become a firm offer when the Department of Defense notified the US Congress of the sale of 11 F-15C/Ds to Israel, with deliveries commencing in April 1985.

The *Peace Fox III* deal covered the supply of nine F-15Cs and two F-15Ds as part of a $510 million contract. This third *Peace Fox* project increased the overall Israeli F-15 purchase to 51 – the 11th jet in this latest deal was an attrition replacement aircraft. This total matched the IDF/AF's original requirement for 50 F-15s as outlined by Beni Peled in 1975. And with this number of jets in service, there were now sufficient F-15s available to support two units.

Accordingly, the Spearhead Squadron's Set-Up Team was activated as an integral part of the Double Tail Squadron in April 1982. The new Baz unit would be equipped with Baz 2 (*Peace Fox II*) and Baz 3 (*Peace Fox III*) jets, and although the former had been delivered from August 1981, the latter were not scheduled to arrive in Israel until April 1985. IDF/AF staff officers decided, therefore, that the new squadron should not be activated before late 1982. However, prospective Spearhead Squadron CO Yoel Feldsho pressed for an earlier activation, and the resulting debate finally ended in a compromise when 6 June 1982 was set as the official unit activation date.

On the very day that the Spearhead Squadron was scheduled to become a separate entity from the Double Tail Squadron, a military clash between the IDF and the PLO disrupted IDF/AF planning. Instead, the Double Tail Squadron fought a brief war from the best possible starting point – a battle proven cadre of pilots equipped with almost 40 jets.

The activation of the second Baz squadron would have to wait another ten days, during which time the Double Tail Squadron was credited with an additional 33 aerial victories.

**Spearhead Squadron maintainers greet their Senior Deputy Commander, Ran Granot, on 19 April 1982 after he had 'ferried' Baz 821 *Peres* (Lammergeyer) to the new unit's Set-Up Team HAS complex at Tel Nof. Shaul Schwartz was credited with a shared MiG-25 kill in this jet on 31 August 1982 to increase the Baz's aerial victory tally for that year to 35.5. This aircraft was lost in an accident on 10 February 1991, killing Baz Conversion Course student Israel Ornan. He was the fifth Baz pilot to lose his life between 1979 and 1991 – a notorious period in the F-15's history, which saw five pilots killed. Several had tried to eject from their aircraft but had failed due to problems with the aircraft's ejection seat and restrictions caused by the pilots' helmet-mounted display**

# LEBANON WAR

On the evening of 3 June 1982, three Arab men approached Israeli Ambassador to the United Kingdom Shlomo Argov as he left a banquet at the Dorchester Hotel, on Park Lane, in the West End of London. One drew a pistol and shot Argov in the head, critically wounding him. In a coma for three months, the ambassador survived the attack, although he would remain paralysed for the rest of his life. The would-be assassins were members of PLO splinter group Fatah-Revolutionary Council, led by notorious terrorist Abu Nidal. Upon discovering the identity of the Arab gunmen, Israel launched a series of retaliatory air strikes against PLO targets in Lebanon within 24 hours of the assassination attempt having taken place.

These air strikes were viewed by the Palestinians as a violation of the July 1981 ceasefire agreement, and they responded by firing dozens of unguided Katyusha rockets at Israeli towns and villages along the Israeli-Lebanese border. Over the next 48 hours, the exchange of fire continued to escalate, resulting in the IDF mobilising reserve units and deploying several armoured divisions along the border. On 6 June, the divisions rumbled north into Lebanon, thus initiating a full-scale invasion.

The IDF immediately announced that the aim of its military action was to establish a 40-kilometre buffer zone inside Lebanon that moved Israeli towns and villages beyond the range of the PLO's artillery and rockets, thus ensuring peace for the country's Galilee region. However, Israel willingly broadened the aims of its offensive following a request for help from its Christian allies in Lebanon. The true objectives of the operation were to cut the Beirut-Damascus highway in the east, capture Beirut in the west, expel the PLO from Lebanon and hand over control of the country to the Christians. The IDF realised that in order to achieve such far reaching goals, it would have to fight Syrian forces in Lebanon.

At first Syria acted with extreme caution, as its government tried to ascertain whether the Israeli offensive was a limited action against the PLO in southern Lebanon or a full-scale war against its occupying forces. And even if the Israeli invasion was exclusively aimed at the destruction of the PLO's infrastructure, Syria had publicly committed itself to the defence of the Palestinians. The SyAAF was duly placed on alert on 4 June, and Syrian fighters flew CAP missions over Lebanon later that day.

During the conflict, the Double Tail Squadron would exclusively fly air-to-air sorties protecting strike aircraft hitting targets located outside the SAM umbrella provided by the Syrian IADS in Lebanon. Baz CAPs were usually flown in four-ship formations, with additional pairs of jets sat at various states of readiness ready to scramble from Tel Nof – up to eight F-15s could man the alert duty in the interception HAS complex.

While the Syrians were busily trying to ascertain the scope of the Israeli offensive, the IDF was struggling to conceal the true objectives of the invasion. Both sides, therefore, were keen to avoid air combat in the early stages of the offensive, and this remained the case until the afternoon of

7 June 1982. Despite military leaders from Syria and Israel doing their level best to avoid an immediate escalation in the fighting, it was only a matter of time before there was a clash between SyAAF and IDF/AF pilots conducting operations in the limited airspace over southern Lebanon. This finally occurred at 1500 hrs local time on the 7th, and Baz pilot Offer Lapidot found himself in the thick of the action;

'We were on a CAP south of Beirut. The Syrian IADS was still intact, and it covered all the area from the Lebanese-Syrian border in the east up to the ridge of the Lebanon Mountains in the west. This meant that in order to stay outside of the IADS' engagement envelope, yet still provide cover for the strike aircraft, we had to patrol over the coast. We received plenty of warning about SyAAF aircraft both from our fighter controllers and the radar screens in our jets. A threat got too close to our attack aircraft and we were vectored in to protect them. The weather was cloudy below us, and we stayed above the undercast throughout the mission.

'For some reason that I cannot now recall, my four-ship formation – in which I was No 4 – lost the target aircraft that we had initially been vectored onto. When we reached the boundary of the IADS engagement envelope we turned back. Just as I completed my turn to the west, I visually acquired a MiG-23 at a range of between five and seven miles. The jet was clearly visible against the clouds behind it, and I could see that the MiG's wings were not swept back. We turned from south to west and the Syrian pilot turned from west to north. I locked my radar onto the MiG-23 and stated over the radio that I had a positive identification, and that I was about to launch an AAM. I duly fired an AIM-7F seconds later.

'The greatest problem facing my squadron during the war was the correct identification of aircraft that we encountered north of the border. The informal order that we obeyed within the unit was that no one was to open fire without first achieving a positive identification of the target. This was just as well, for later in the war I intercepted a jet and the GCU cleared me to fire an AAM, but I chose not launch the missile. This was a wise move, as it turned out that my "target" was an IDF/AF aircraft!

'The Sparrow failed to hit the MiG-23, despite it meeting all the required acquisition parameters that included the target being well within its engagement envelope. By the time I realised that I had missed, I was within Python 3 range of the jet. I therefore fired a single WVR AAM at a distance of 1.5 miles whilst flying at an altitude of 1000-2000 ft in a look-down position on the MiG, which made it more difficult for the missile to track its target. Soon after firing the weapon I turned sharply to the east in order to avoid any SAMs, or an engagement with the MiG-23's wingman. This in turn meant that I did not see the AAM hit the target. Other pilots in my formation saw the kill, however.'

Double Tail Squadron EP pilot Offer Lapidot was flying Baz 658

Devoid of any external stores, Baz 658 (F-15A 76-1506) *Typhoon* departs Tel Nof in afterburner during a May 1985 scramble demonstration. Double Tail Squadron's EP Offer Lapidot was flying this jet when he was credited with the Baz's first aerial victory of the Lebanon War on 7 June 1982. Two days later Gil Rapaport claimed a MiG-23 destroyed with an AIM-7F fired from Baz 658

when he claimed the first aerial kill of the Lebanon War. Two days later, Baz 658 would be credited with its second victory, and on 11 June Offer Lapidot claimed his second kill, which ultimately proved to be the last aerial victory credited to the Double Tail Squadron during this conflict. Sandwiched between Lapidot's kills were 31 victories for the Baz.

On 8 June IDF/AF strike aircraft began a systematic bombing campaign that targeted Syrian troop emplacements in Lebanon, with the sites that were attacked being specifically chosen because they were located outside the engagement envelope of the Syrian IADS. However, this escalation in the fighting triggered an immediate response from the SyAAF, which began utilising audio communication jamming equipment to disrupt IDF/AF F-15s and F-16s that were attempting to vector onto Arab jets sent to intercept Israeli attack aircraft.

The Baz pilots reacted by minimising their audio communication, releasing chaff and splitting the customary four-ship CAP formations in half once the GCU order to engage was received – two pairs of F-15s operating independently of one another were harder for the Syrians to track than a single formation of four jets.

Overall, the Israeli tactics worked better than those employed by their opponents during two of the five engagements between F-15s and Syrian aircraft on 8 June. The first of these encounters took place in the morning, when a two-aircraft Baz CAP operating with the call-sign 'Palace' was vectored onto SyAAF jets detected in the Beirut sector. Flying east of the Lebanese capital, 'Palace 2' (Yoram Hoffman in Baz 686) locked onto a target flying at a lower altitude 15 miles east of the city.

Obeying the instruction that all interceptions should be WVR rather than BVR, the 'Palace' formation continued to close on the SyAAF jets. Finally, at a range of less than five miles, Shaul Schwartz in 'Palace 1' (F-15B 957, with navigator Reuven Solan in the back seat) acquired the enemy aircraft within his HUD Target Designation Box (TDB). It appears that the MiG-21 pilots may very well have detected the F-15s at this point, as they made a sharp banking turn to the left and headed south, only to be followed by the 'Palace' jets. Both Baz pilots fired a single AIM-7F at a range of two miles as the enemy aircraft attempted to accelerate away. Seconds later both MiG-21s fell in flames.

The second Baz interception on 8 June came several hours later when Shaul Simon (in Baz 818) shared a MiG-23 kill with his wingman Dedi Rosenthal (in Baz 832), both pilots having simultaneously launched single AIM-7Fs at the jet.

That same day, Netz pilots had been credited with three kills between the two Baz engagements.

## IADS SUPPRESSION

Israeli jets shot down seven SyAAF MiG-21s and MiG-23s during the first 72 hours of the Lebanon War, yet the IDF/AF's greatest achieve-

A groundcrewman from the Spearhead Squadron conducts routine maintenance in the cockpit of Baz 818 *Tamnoon* (Octopus) whilst the jet is parked inside one of the unit's HASs at Tel Nof in 2003. For many years this aircraft was erroneously marked with two victory symbols, although by the time this photograph was taken these had been removed – note the area of darker grey paint just above the jet's name. A new kill tally consisting of 1.5 SyAAF roundels was applied instead, as seen here. Even the new version is still on the optimistic side, however, as Baz 818 was only ever credited with sharing in the destruction of a MiG-23 whilst being flown by Shaul Simon on 8 June 1982

ment was not in securing aerial supremacy, but in neutralising the IADS threat through a series of highly successful SEAD missions. The superiority of the F-15 and F-16 over the MiG-21, MiG-23 and MiG-25 had already been proven during the skirmishes of 1979-81, and this had a direct impact on the air war in June 1982, as Offer Lapidot explained;

'A typical engagement during the Lebanon War was a vector to engage, radar acquisition of the enemy aircraft, lock-on, visual identification, a turn and AAM launch. Sometimes the weapons missed, but on most occasions they hit. There was no dogfighting for Baz and Netz pilots.'

An awareness of this superiority had been the motivation behind the Syrians moving a multi-layered IADS into Lebanon in April-May 1981. The presence of the latter meant that for the IDF/AF to achieve air superiority over Lebanon, it had to first destroy the IADS, rather than simply clearing the skies of MiGs. The IDF/AF duly prepared tactics, EW equipment and weapons to challenge the SAM network, having learned the bitter lessons of its failed SEAD effort in the Yom Kippur War.

While the IDF/AF was ready to challenge the Syrian IADS, the decision to launch this phase of the campaign was not an easy one to take. The Lebanon War was only a limited conflict in comparison with previous wars in the Middle East, and senior officers in the IDF were concerned that a successful SEAD operation would give Israel's enemies the chance to develop systems and tactics that negated the IDF/AF's EW advantage. A compromise proposal put forward to target only one or two SAM batteries as a warning to the Syrians was rejected, and on 9 June 1982, the Israeli government approved an all out SEAD offensive.

Operation *Artzav* (Mole Cricket) proved to be an overwhelming success, with the IDF/AF claiming the destruction of 14 SAM batteries without a single loss in return. And although the Baz pilots only flew CAP missions during the war, they directly benefited from the successful SEAD operation, as in a frantic effort to rescue the IADS from total destruction, the SyAAF scrambled dozens of interceptors. This proved to be a fatal mistake by the Syrian leadership, for the losses suffered in the air only served to magnify the margin of the Israeli victory.

In addition to the destruction of the IADS in Lebanon on 9 June, the IDF/AF claimed 25 jets shot down – 11 were credited to Baz pilots.

Ronen Shapira claimed the first kill on the 9th when he destroyed a MiG-21 whilst on a morning CAP between Beirut and Rayak – this mission was flown some hours before the SEAD operation commenced at 1400 hrs local time. Shapira, who was flying Baz 684, recalled the first of his three 9 June missions in an interview conducted in 1988;

'I was No 4 on a CAP when our GCU reported enemy aircraft flying some 35 miles from us, southeast of Beirut. We headed towards them, and at a range of 20 miles I locked onto a jet that was flying at low altitude in a westerly direction at 650 knots. I reported this to my formation leader, who in turn handed me the mission lead.

'At a range of six miles, the target crossed my flight path, before turning right and heading east. I could not identify the aircraft until I was at a range of less than 2500 metres, at which point I finally saw that my opponent was a Syrian MiG-23. The fighter was off to my left, flying east in full afterburner, so I pulled 6G and closed up behind him. At a range of 1500 metres, I achieved radar lock onto the target and launched a single

**Baz 684 was a *Peace Fox* jet that had seen ten years of service with the IDF/AF when it was lost in a mid-air collision during an ACMI training mission on 15 August 1988 while being flown by Double Tail Squadron CO Ram Caller. Named *Ha Arpad* (The Vampire) in 1981, Baz 684 was credited with two kills on 9 June 1982. Ronen Shapira claimed a MiG-23 during a morning CAP and Yoram Peled destroyed a MiG-21 whilst on an afternoon patrol. Baz 684 bore three victory symbols at the time of its crash, thus proving once again the fallibility of the IDF/AF's kill markings system**

AIM-7F. The missile flew off into nearby clouds, so I immediately launched a second AAM, but then I spotted the first weapon again and tracked it until it hit the MiG – the second Sparrow flew straight into the fireball caused by the explosion of the first missile.'

A few minutes later Gil Rapaport (in Baz 658) was also destroyed a MiG-23. That afternoon, three Baz formations would claim nine more victories during four engagements – two of these were 'no weapon' unit kills. This classification harked back to the early days of the IDF/AF, when 'no weapon' kills were credited to the squadron even if the aircraft's destruction was directly attributable to the actions of an Israeli pilot.

However, from the mid-1970s onwards, the IDF/AF's attitude towards 'no weapon' kill credits changed whereby the victory would be re-designated a 'manoeuvre kill'. This in turn was credited to the pilot who caused his opponent to either lose control and crash or fly into the ground. Nevertheless, there were still certain air combat scenarios that resulted in the destruction of an enemy aircraft, but not in the award of a personal kill certificate to the pilot involved.

Just such an engagement was fought at noon on 9 June, when a Baz formation was vectored onto two MiG-21s. The Israeli pilots had acquired their targets visually and were preparing to attack when their two Syrian opponents unwittingly flew into clouds that shrouded a mountain ridge. Both men perished in the ensuing crash, and since none of the F-15 pilots had posed a specific threat to the MiG-21s prior to them hitting the ridge, they were classified as 'no weapon' unit kills.

There was no disputing the victors of the next four kills, which fell in short order to a four-ship formation led by Moshe Melnik (in Baz 802) that was involved in near back-to-back engagements. The Baz pilots initially intercepted two MiG-23s, with each F-15 pair being allotted a target. Melnik downed his 'Flogger-G' with an AIM-7F, and when the pilot in the No 3 Baz suffered a technical malfunction, the No 4 pilot, Avi Maor (in Baz 646), launched a Python 3 that hit the MiG-23. And just when Maor thought that his missile had failed to damage the Syrian jet, he suddenly saw its pilot eject. Having downed both MiG-23s, the Baz formation turned west to resume its CAP.

Unlike the IDF/AF's previous generation of jet fighters such as the Phantom II and Mirage IIIC, the

Baz 802 *Panther* was the first of the nine *Peace Fox II* F-15Cs to be delivered to the IDF/AF. The aircraft was adorned with four kill markings after the Lebanon War to commemorate the two victories that Moshe Melnik had achieved on 9 June 1982 and the pair of MiG-23s destroyed by Noam Knaani the very next day. The aircraft is seen here after suffering a landing incident at Tel Nof in May 1994 – it was soon repaired and returned to flying status. *Panther* is the IDF/AF's second highest scoring Baz, a title it shares with Baz 646

45

F-15 had plenty of fuel to continue flying its CAP after a brief aerial engagement like the one fought by Melnik's flight. Crews flying the F-4 or Mirage IIIC rarely returned to their CAP station following a clash with enemy fighters because their older jets had less fuel to burn, and they also consumed it at a greater rate since their aerodynamic and weapon system performance were on a par with enemy MiGs. This in turn meant that they had to dogfight, and this was usually when fuel burn was at its worst.

The Baz's superiority over SyAAF fighters was so profound that air combat in June 1982 bore no resemblance to the engagements of 1973.

Whilst heading back to its CAP station, Melnik's formation was bounced by two MiG-21s, which launched AAMs at the Nos 3 and 4 jets. Luckily for the Israelis, the missiles failed to guide, but it was a very, very close call. In the ensuing melee, Melnik downed a MiG-21 with a Python 3 and Maor destroyed the second jet with cannon fire. This victory was the first of only two cannon kills credited to the Baz in the Lebanon War.

Although Melnik's formation had had a narrow escape, the closest call for a Baz pilot in the war came during the very next engagement of 9 June.

By the time Yoram Peled led a four-ship CAP formation from Tel Nof at 1730 hrs, the Syrian IADS in the Lebanon Valley had already been badly degraded following the launch of Operation *Artzav*.

Accompanying Peled on this fateful mission were Ronen Shapira, Eitan Ben-Eliyahu and Oran Hampel. The formation flew north over the Mediterranean Sea and then turned east, crossing the Lebanon Mountain ridge and heading into the Lebanon Valley. Here, it conducted a CAP over Rayak until GCU vectored the formation south to intercept Syrian fighters that had been detected some 20 miles away. Closing to within three miles of the contacts, Ben-Eliyahu was the first to visually acquire two MiG-21s, which in turn made him formation leader.

With the rear pair of F-15s now in the lead, Ben-Eliyahu and his wingman Hampel (in Baz 695) each launched an AAM. The latter pilot watched his AIM-7F hit the MiG, which burst into flames – only the forward fuselage could be seen ahead of the fireball, and as the fighter lost height, Hampel spotted his Syrian counterpart ejecting from the cockpit.

Ben-Eliyahu had not enjoyed the same level of success with his missile, having to violently manoeuvre his jet so as to avoid an accurate burst of AAA, thus breaking the Sparrow's radar lock on its target. The Syrian's good fortune did not last long, however, for Yoram Peled (in Baz 684) downed the MiG-21 with a Python 3. By then the whole area was alive with fiery ribbons of AAA, and GCU ordered the Baz pilots to disengage.

Seconds prior to the disengagement order being issued, a MiG-21 shot across the nose of Ronen Shapira's Baz 686. The two jets were barely 200 metres apart at the time, and the pilots simply looked at each other as they flashed past at a combined closing speed of nearly 1000 mph. Having heard the call to disengage, Shapira was in the process of rejoining the remaining three Bazs when his Syrian opponent completed a perfect turning manoeuvre that placed his MiG-21 right behind Baz 686.

Spotting the SyAAF jet on his tail, Shapira slowed his F-15 down and then pulled into a high-G turn of his own that ended with him sat aft of the Syrian fighter. The first AAM that he fired missed the MiG-21, but the second Python 3 struck its target. However, the jet did not explode, but instead lost height whilst trailing a plume of white smoke.

It was at this critical moment that Ben-Eliyahu joined the fight, and Shapira, who was determined to make sure that the kill was his alone, followed the MiG-21 down until it hit the ground and exploded. By choosing to stay with the MiG-21, Shapira had traded his situational awareness for kill verification, and this was almost his undoing. Seconds after the SyAAF jet had crashed, an AAM fired by an unseen Syrian fighter exploded inside the right-hand engine nozzle of Baz 686, destroying the F100 turbofan engine and starting a fire.

Ronen Shapira was the son of Danny Shapira, who was flying Meteor F8s with the IDF/AF at the time of Ronen's birth. Shapira senior later attended the French Air Force's EPNER test pilots' school from 1958, and he eventually became the IDF/AF's Chief Test Pilot. In 1970 he joined IAI as its Chief Test Pilot, and he served in this capacity until 1984. Ronen junior followed in his father's footsteps, graduating from Flying School Class 73 in 1974 and eventually being posted to a fighter squadron. He had completed the US Navy Test Pilots' School course just prior to the Lebanon War, and he joined IAI as a test pilot soon after the conflict ended. Ronen Shapira has been IAI's Chief Test pilot since 2004.

Twenty-two years earlier, on 9 June 1982, Shapira needed all of his piloting skills to coax his crippled jet back home. His F-15 was on fire and struggling at low altitude through heavy AAA on just one engine. Shapira switched off the rapidly overheating right turbofan and applied full power to the functioning F100. Avoiding the AAA, he slowly climbed up to 17,000 ft, which was just high enough to clear the peaks of the Lebanon Mountains, before heading west towards the Mediterranean Sea.

Accompanying Shapira throughout this ordeal was Yoram Peled, who maintained station off his left wing, Eitan Ben-Eliyahu, who was off his right wing, and Oran Hampel, who trailed behind all three F-15s and guarded the tail of the damaged jet. Upon crossing the Lebanese coastline, Shapira decided that he would be able to nurse the jet to Ramat David, which was the IDF/AF's northernmost base.

A 'normal' single engine approach and landing was duly made, followed by a somewhat hair-raising stop using the jet's landing arrestor gear. The latter was torn off the F-15 shortly after it caught the raised runway barrier, and Ronen Shapira decided not to apply the brakes so as to avoid generating more friction that could in turn add further heat to the already burning jet. The damaged Baz eventually rolled into the emergency netting at the end of the runway and stopped. Ramat David's firefighting crews quickly extinguished the fire in the right engine, thus allowing Shapira to make a preliminary inspection of the damage.

The right F100 engine was wrecked, the left one had also suffered some splinter damage and there were hundreds of holes all over the horizontal and vertical stabilisers. A fire had consumed the underbelly of the jet, the conflagration having been fed by fuel leaking from a ruptured tank in the right wing. Despite looking worse for wear, Baz 686 had survived thanks to the F-15's reliance on two powerful engines. The jet was back in the air within two months, sporting two kill markings beneath its cockpit.

### 10 JUNE 1982

10 June provided the Double Tail Squadron with its best day of the conflict in terms of aerial kills, with 13 aircraft being shot down.

**Ronen Shapira (right) flew his father Daniel in Baz 280 (F-15D 83-0064) *Yad Ha Nefetz* (Shatter Hand) in 1987, the latter having served in the IDF/AF as a fighter pilot from 1948 to 1958. In that time he had seen operational service with the Spitfire, P-51D, Mosquito, Meteor, Ouragan and Mystere, prior to then pursuing a new career as a test pilot. Shapira senior was fortunate enough not to have to bale out or eject during his long flying career. His son Ronen inherited his father's flying abilities, as well as his good luck, and both were put to the test on 9 June 1982 when he flew badly damaged Baz 686 back to Tel Nof after it had suffered an AAM strike**

Opposing troops clashed in the Lebanon Valley south of the Beirut-Damascus highway throughout the course of the day, and with the IADS in Lebanon no longer functioning, it was up to SyAAF jets to try and protect Syrian troops on the ground from air strikes by IDF/AF fighter-bombers. Arab strike aircraft and attack helicopters also attempted to hit IDF positions and armoured columns on the 10th.

The Baz pilots' tasking remained the same, but now they were escorting jets all over Lebanon due to the removal of the IADS threat.

Avner Naveh, with navigator Michael Cohen in the backseat of Baz 957, opened the scoring with two MiG-23s and a MiG-21 destroyed during the course of a single sortie. This trio of kills made Naveh the world's first F-15 ace, as he had previously claimed two MiG-21s on 24 September 1979 – he also has the distinction of being the only Israeli to claim three kills in a single sortie with the Baz. A short while later Ziv Nadivi (in Baz 848) claimed the aircraft's only non-MiG kill of the war when he downed a Gazelle with a Python 3 AAM to prove that the F-15 was also capable of knocking down low and slow targets such as helicopters.

The F-15's mastery of Lebanese skies was so complete that pilots flying the aircraft believed that in order to achieve a kill you simply had to be in the right place at the right time. Everyone was eager to take on the SyAAF, but in an effort to spread the workload, missions were allocated as evenly as possible. Operational procedures within the unit dictated that formation leaders and pair leaders flew the most due to their experience in the aircraft, but relatively junior pilots flying as wingmen still got plenty of sorties under their belts. And some pilots soon gained a reputation for being 'luckier' than others when it came to scoring kills.

Moshe Melnik always considered himself to be a 'lucky' pilot, as he seemed to be in the right place at the right time far more frequently than most of his contemporaries. One of the first five Israeli pilots to transition onto the F-15, he was credited with the jet's first aerial kill, he assumed command of the Double Tail Squadron in time to lead the Osirak raid and, to date, he is the only Israeli to have led a Baz unit in wartime.

Mickey Lev, who was the Double Tail Squadron's senior deputy commander, felt quite the opposite to his CO. Indeed, it seemed that whenever he entered Lebanese airspace the MiGs simply vanished.

Fully aware that Lev was desperate to claim a kill, Melnik decided to share his luck with his second-in-command on 10 June. He assembled a

Baz 667 (F-15A 76-1509) was named *Cyclone* from 1981 and credited with a single air-to-air kill on 10 March 1982 when Double Tail Squadron EP pilot Yiftach Shadmi shot down a MiG-21 while flying as wingman to Yoram Peled and Zvi Lipsitz in Baz 979. Seen here in the 1990s, Baz 667 has had red trim applied to the leading edges of its wings as part of a DACT exercise

CAP formation, and had Lev fill the sub-leader's position in the No 3 slot. Melnik's lucky streak continued, for the MiGs duly appeared, and Lev (flying alone in two-seat Baz 955) destroyed a MiG-21 with a Python 3.

Hypnotised by the exploding jet in front of him, Lev failed to break away in time and Baz 955 was hit by debris, which fractured its canopy. However, as had been proven the previous day, the Baz was capable of withstanding such punishment, and Lev made it safely home.

Yoram Peled was another 'lucky' Baz pilot, and he recalled;

'All of my missions were flown according to the operational schedule created by the squadron, and I was fortunate enough to see combat during almost every one of them in June 1982. Other pilots also deemed me to be lucky too, and from my fourth sortie onwards my squadronmates began to ask me if they could join my formation. I was a senior leader in the unit, and had already downed two MiGs since the war had started. Pilots who had not seen an enemy fighter in the air were getting desperate in the quest to claim a kill before the conflict ended.'

Ronen Shapira was another 'lucky' Baz pilot, and just a day after surviving being hit by an AAM, he claimed his third kill whilst flying in the backseat of Baz 708. The man 'sat up front' was Shaul Schwartz, who fired the Python 3 that hit a MiG-21 over the Lebanon Valley – this was Schwartz's second kill of the war, and both had come in F-15Bs. This victory gave Shapira the unique distinction of being the only Baz pilot to claim kills while flying both in the front and back seats of the F-15.

## 11 JUNE 1982

The IDF was only a few kilometres short of achieving its objectives when a ceasefire came into effect at 1200 hrs on 11 June. The vanguard of the ground force was still south of Beirut, the Beirut-Damascus highway had not yet been cutoff and the Christian militia's enclave north of Beirut had not yet been reached. These objectives would be achieved over coming weeks, however, in a series of bloody skirmishes east of Beirut.

The intensity of the aerial activity decreased on the 11th, although Baz pilots still managed to claim five kills on the last day of the Lebanon War.

Two of these fell to 'lucky' pilot Yoram Peled, who was leading a four-ship formation with the call-sign 'Adulthood' on a morning CAP. The pilots flying with Peled were Udi Zohar, Avner Naveh and Noam Knaani, who had claimed two MiG-23s kills the previous day.

Baz 979 *Mashak Knafaim* (Wings Wave) was the sixth, and last, *Peace Fox II* F-15D delivered to the IDF/AF. It was credited with three kills during 1982, Yoram Peled and Zvi Lipsitz claiming a MiG-21 destroyed on 10 June 1982 when the jet was assigned to the Double Tail Squadron, and Yoel Feldsho and Zvi Lipsitz downing two MiG-23s exactly two weeks later, by which point the F-15D had been reassigned to the Spearhead Squadron. In this 1993 view, Baz 979 is equipped with a Popeye ASM training round

Proving the F-15's ability to autonomously track high-flying targets as well as aircraft at low-level, Peled locked onto a jet cruising at 63,000 ft some 90 miles away from 'Adulthood' soon after the formation crossed into Lebanon. He passed on the target data to GCU and awaited their instructions, and he was eventually told to ignore the contact and press on to his CAP station. Peled later found out that a USAF U-2 was monitoring the fighting on the ground in the lead up to the ceasefire.

Fifteen minutes later, the good fortune that always seemed to be with Yoram Peled whenever he ventured into Lebanon saw him receive a target vector after enemy jets had been detected over Rayak. Shortly after crossing the coast north of Beirut, 'Adulthood 2' acquired targets heading east at a range of 25 miles. Seconds later, the Baz formation leader visually identified them as a pair of low-flying MiG-23s. Yoram Peled recalled;

'The AIM-7F had proven to be a disappointment when fired head-on at a target, so we decided not to use this weapon in such engagements. The Sparrow had also been less than reliable in lookdown interceptions, when the AAM was tasked with hitting a jet during a low-altitude pursuit.

'On this particular occasion, I had no other alternative but to fire an AIM-7F in lookdown shoot down mode. I was chasing two MiG-23s that were being flown very fast at low altitude. I got to within two miles of the trailing jet, but could get no closer. This meant that the aircraft were too far away for me to use a Python 3, so I launched an AIM-7F without thinking that it would hit the target. My luck held, however, and it hit the MiG-23 in the tail. Pleased with this result, I wasted no time in firing off a second Sparrow missile, which destroyed the lead jet.'

These two victories made Yoram Peled the second Baz ace. Indeed, to date only he and Avner Naveh have achieved ace status exclusively with the F-15. Moshe Melnik was already a 5.5-kill ace when he claimed three victories with the Baz, whilst Relik Shafir scored his first kill as an F-15 pilot and went on to 'make ace' in the Netz during the Lebanon War.

With fewer enemy aircraft to shoot down over the past 30 years, the Baz has struggled to emulate the feats of the Mirage IIIC and Nesher, which destroyed almost 400 aircraft between them and created nearly 40 aces. The IDF/AF F-4E force claimed 116.5 kills and boasted seven aces. To date, the Baz has destroyed 50 aircraft and produced two aces.

As previously mentioned, Offer Lapidot claimed the first Baz kill of the Lebanon War, and on the afternoon of 11 June 1982, whilst flying as a wingman in Baz 646, he also got the campaign's last victory. He recalled;

'We were flying a CAP over the Mediterranean Sea. Following the destruction of the IADS, we had almost total freedom of flight over

**Yoram Peled was flying Baz 678 (F-15A 76-1514)** *Ha Yoreh* **(The Shooter) when he was credited with two MiG-23 kills on 11 June 1982 that made him the world's second, and so far last, F-15 ace**

Lebanon. We were eventually vectored east towards Lake Karoun, in the Lebanon Valley, and as we closed on the contact we found that our radar lock kept fluctuating. We flew head-on towards each other, the Syrian pilots being at a lower altitude than us. Minutes later, we flashed past each other, so my leader and I pulled into a high-G turn and headed back in a westerly direction immediately behind the fighters. I quickly acquired a target on my radar and pointed my nose at the enemy jets – we were chasing two MiG-21s that were speeding along at low altitude.

'They soon turned right onto an easterly heading, and although I was less than one mile behind the trailing jet, the boresight angle was at the limit of the launch envelope for my AAM. The first Python 3 that I fired missed, but the second missile scored a direct hit. As with my first kill four days earlier, I did not see the jet crash, as I had quickly reversed direction in order to search for the second MiG-21. However, my leader saw the pilot ejecting from the jet that I had shot down.'

The Double Tail Squadron had flown 316 sorties during the Lebanon War, all of them optimised exclusively for the air-to-air mission mostly in the form of CAPs – a number of scrambles to intercept unknown contacts had also been carried out. The unit was credited with 33 kills and no losses, although three jets were damaged, including one extensively. Except for a handful of BVR interceptions, Baz pilots had stuck exclusively to WVR intercepts as per the IDF/AF rules of engagement, which were quite conservative throughout the campaign.

Of the 33 kills credited to the jet, 29 were scored with AAMs. Only two had been achieved with the aircraft's 20 mm cannon, and two more were 'no weapon' kills credited to the squadron. As for the 29 missile kills, the leading weapon employed was the IR-guided Rafael Python 3, which accounted for 19 of the victories. The remaining ten were credited to the SARH AIM-7F.

Interestingly, the IR-to-SARH AAM kill ratio that stood at 1-to-5 prior to the initiation of the SEAD offensive at 1400 hrs local time on 9 June 1982 had changed to 18-to-5 once the IADS threat was removed.

Double Tail Squadron CO Moshe Melnik summed up his unit's achievements as follows;

'We fought well and ended the war without any losses due to the survivability of the Baz . . . and a little bit of luck.'

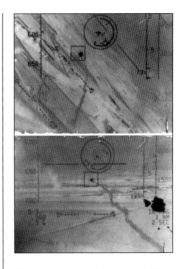

These photographs from Baz 678's HUD camera reveal the precise moments when the two AIM-7Fs fired by Yoram Peled destroyed two MiG-23s on 11 June 1982. For the first kill (top), Peled was flying at an altitude of 3350 ft at almost 600 knots, whilst for the second victory (above) he had descended to 1900 ft and accelerated to 620 knots

The 33 pilots and three navigators of the Double Tail Squadron pose for an 'end of war' photograph at Tel Nof in late June 1982. Behind them are two jets adorned with four kill markings apiece – Baz 695 *Ha Kochav* (The Star) in Double Tail Squadron markings and Baz 802 *Panther* in Spearhead Squadron markings. These aircrew were credited with 33 aerial victories between 7 and 11 June 1982

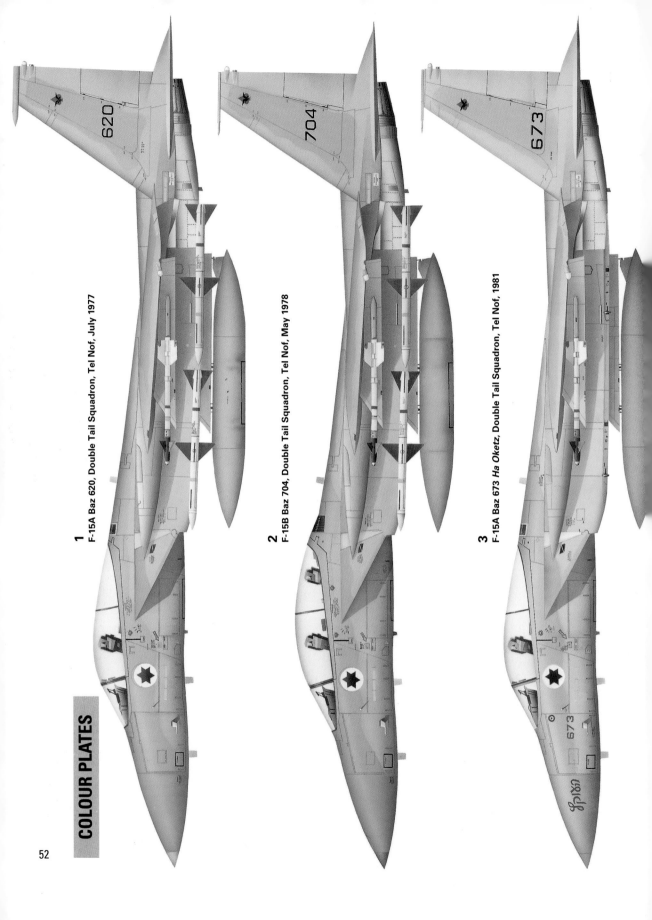

**COLOUR PLATES**

**1**
F-15A Baz 620, Double Tail Squadron, Tel Nof, July 1977

**2**
F-15B Baz 704, Double Tail Squadron, Tel Nof, May 1978

**3**
F-15A Baz 673 *Ha Oketz*, Double Tail Squadron, Tel Nof, 1981

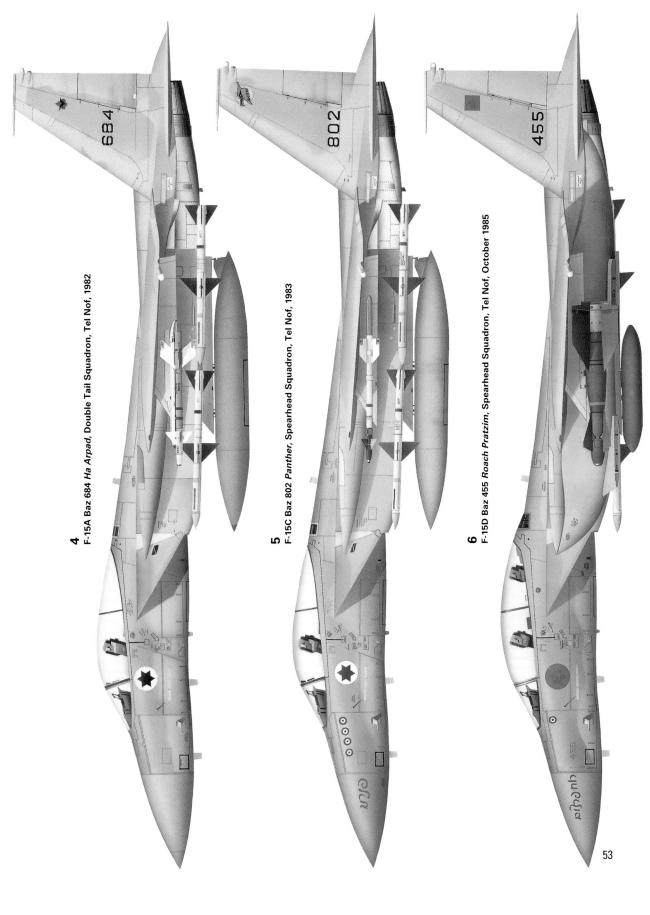

**4**
F-15A Baz 684 *Ha Arpad*, Double Tail Squadron, Tel Nof, 1982

**5**
F-15C Baz 802 *Panther*, Spearhead Squadron, Tel Nof, 1983

**6**
F-15D Baz 455 *Roach Pratzim*, Spearhead Squadron, Tel Nof, October 1985

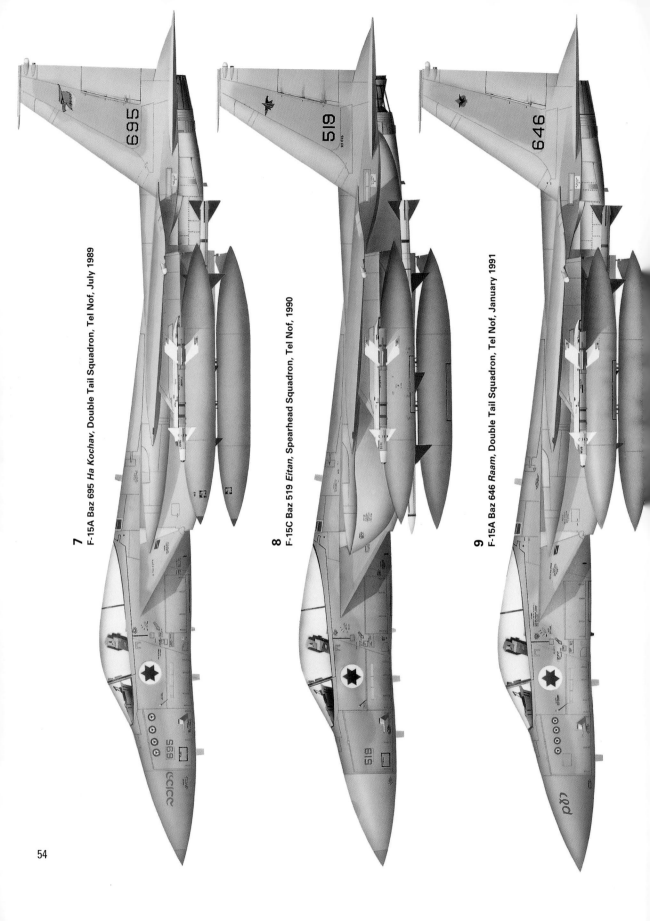

**7**
F-15A Baz 695 *Ha Kochav*, Double Tail Squadron, Tel Nof, July 1989

**8**
F-15C Baz 519 *Eitan*, Spearhead Squadron, Tel Nof, 1990

**9**
F-15A Baz 646 *Raam*, Double Tail Squadron, Tel Nof, January 1991

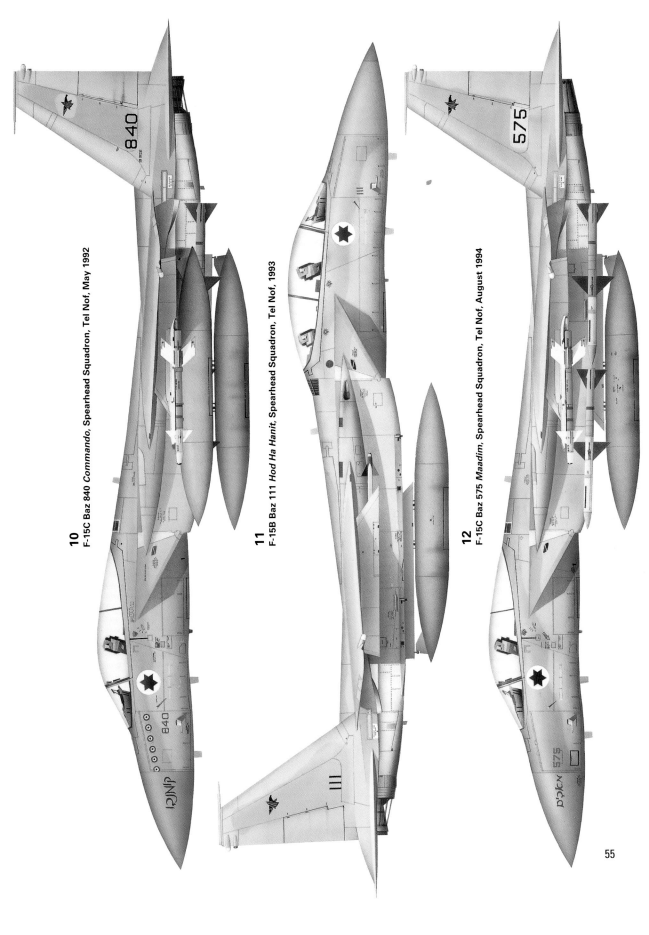

**10**
F-15C Baz 840 *Commando*, Spearhead Squadron, Tel Nof, May 1992

**11**
F-15B Baz 111 *Hod Ha Hanit*, Spearhead Squadron, Tel Nof, 1993

**12**
F-15C Baz 575 *Maadim*, Spearhead Squadron, Tel Nof, August 1994

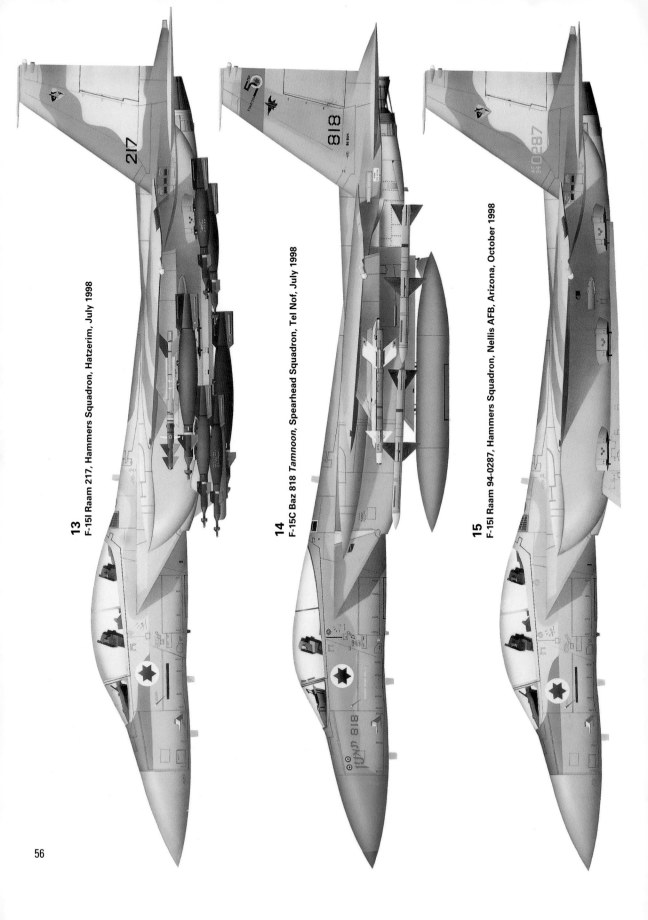

**13**
F-15I Raam 217, Hammers Squadron, Hatzerim, July 1998

**14**
F-15C Baz 818 *Tamnoon*, Spearhead Squadron, Tel Nof, July 1998

**15**
F-15I Raam 94-0287, Hammers Squadron, Nellis AFB, Arizona, October 1998

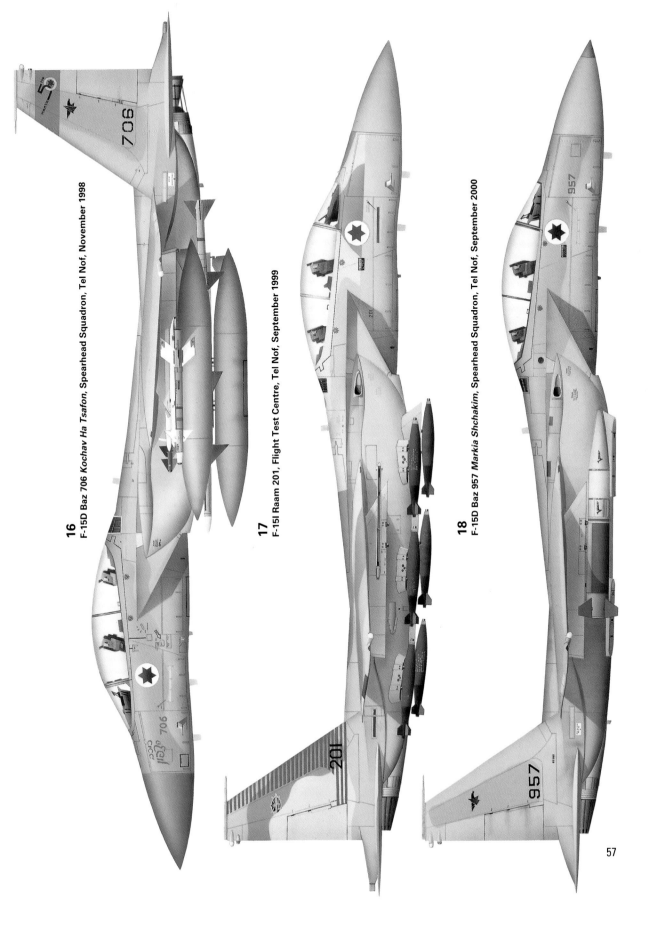

**16**
F-15D Baz 706 *Kochav Ha Tsafon*, Spearhead Squadron, Tel Nof, November 1998

**17**
F-15I Raam 201, Flight Test Centre, Tel Nof, September 1999

**18**
F-15D Baz 957 *Markia Shchakim*, Spearhead Squadron, Tel Nof, September 2000

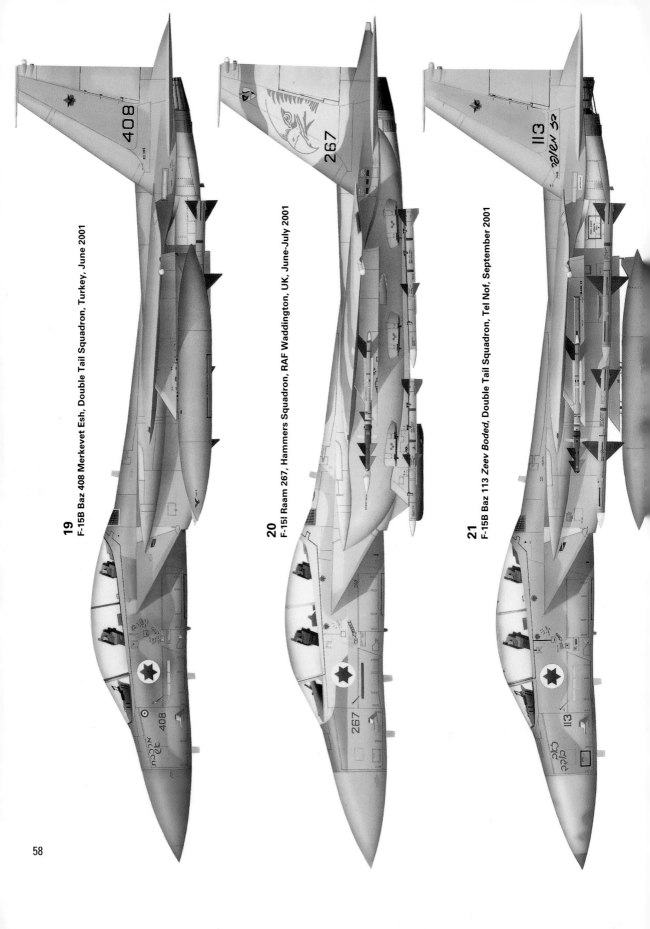

**19**

F-15B Baz 408 Merkevet Esh, Double Tail Squadron, Turkey, June 2001

**20**

F-15I Raam 267, Hammers Squadron, RAF Waddington, UK, June–July 2001

**21**

F-15B Baz 113 *Zeev Boded*, Double Tail Squadron, Tel Nof, September 2001

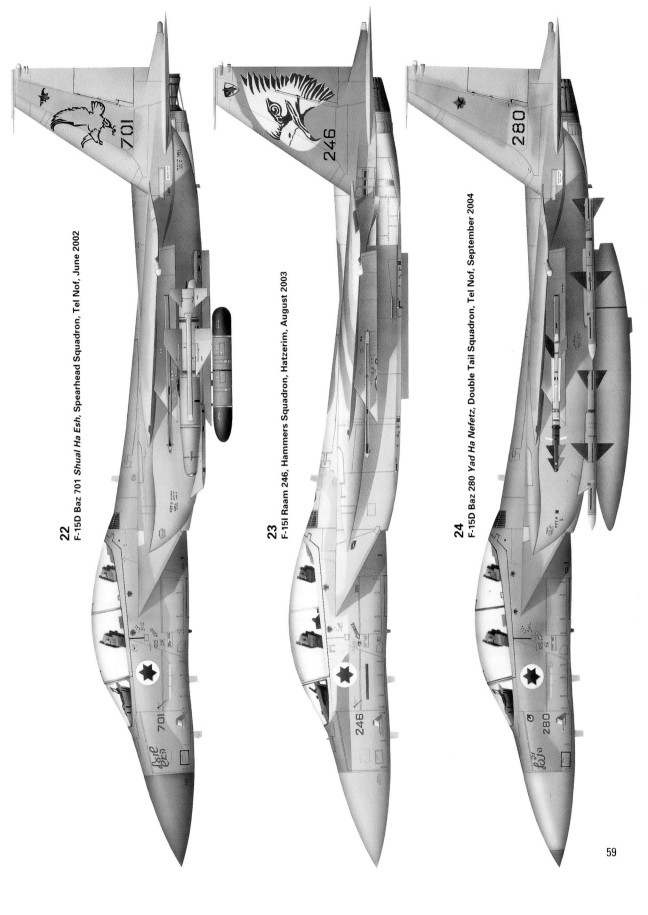

**22**
F-15D Baz 701 *Shual Ha Esh*, Spearhead Squadron, Tel Nof, June 2002

**23**
F-15I Raam 246, Hammers Squadron, Hatzerim, August 2003

**24**
F-15D Baz 280 *Yad Ha Nefetz*, Double Tail Squadron, Tel Nof, September 2004

**1**
Double Tail Squadron
(inner surfaces of vertical stabilisers)

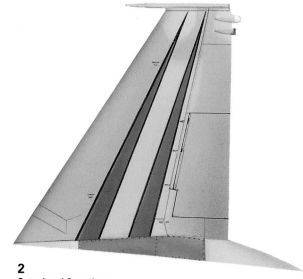

**2**
Spearhead Squadron
(inner surfaces of vertical stabilisers)

**3**
Spearhead Squadron

**4**
Double Tail Squadron

**5**
Double Tail Squadron
(display jet)

**6**
IDF/AF Flight Test Centre

**7**
Hammers Squadron

**8**
Hammers Squadron

# FROM LEBANON TO IRAQ

The summer of 1982 had seen the F-15 cement its place in Israeli folklore. In the decade that preceded the Lebanon War, the IDF/AF managed to introduce the aircraft into service despite diplomatic, monetary and political obstacles. And for the first time in its short history, the IDF/AF possessed a fighter that was a generation ahead of its potential opponents in the Middle East.

Within just six years, the elite Double Tail Squadron had established the Baz's reputation as the world's best fighter, with an unprecedented 45.5-to-0 kills-to-losses ratio. The F-15 had been proven in combat against attack helicopters and jet fighters, thus living up to Israeli hopes for the jet when it was selected for purchase in the early 1970s.

The Israeli fourth generation fighter force grew still further in 1980 with the introduction of the F-16 into frontline service. Although still the best all-round fighter in the IDF/AF, the Baz was no longer the ultimate WVR platform in the Middle East, as the Netz boasted unmatched manoeuvrability. Along with the arrival of the F-16 came more F-15s, and the long awaited establishment of a second Baz squadron.

The growth of the IDF/AF's fourth generation fighter force from a single unit in early 1980 to six squadrons in 1990 also facilitated a broadening of the Baz's operational repertoire which saw the jet metamorphose from being a single mission air-to-air platform into a multi-role combat aircraft, albeit with a distinct air superiority flavour.

Key to this change was the establishment of the Spearhead Squadron on 16 June 1982 – some ten days later than was originally planned. The unit activation ceremony was an austere affair, with IDF/AF commander David Ivry and Tel Nof base commander Yiftach Spector both being in attendance. The 'birth' of the Spearhead Squadron went smoothly thanks to work carried out by the unit's Set-Up Team, which had been active

**Although of poor quality, this photograph is of enormous historical significance as it shows a three-ship of Spearhead Squadron jets preparing to take-off from Tel Nof in late June 1982 – just days after the unit had been established. The fighters, including Baz 832 *Ha Shishi Be Yuni* (The Sixth Of June) and Baz 848 *Baz* (Buzzard), are adorned with an early iteration of the Spearhead Squadron's badge**

within the 'mother' Double Tail Squadron for many months prior to 16 June. Indeed, the team's jets, aircrew and groundcrew had made a major contribution to the latter squadron's success in the Lebanon War.

This in turn meant that all of the Spearhead Squadron's initial cadre of personnel were combat veterans, and nine of the jets assigned to the new unit were already adorned with kill markings. This experience allowed the squadron to achieve initial operational capability in practically no time at all, and the first Spearhead Squadron mission was flown on 22 June 1982 from 'Baz Land' – the popular name for the area within Tel Nof air base where the two F-15 squadrons were located.

The Lebanon War officially ended with a ceasefire on 11 June 1982, although hostilities were in fact far from over. The Israelis had not yet achieved their military objectives, so the IDF launched a series of offensives that 'crept' east of Beirut towards the Beirut-Damascus highway. Finally, once troops had cut off this crucial transport link between the PLO and Syria, and linked up with the Christian militia north of Beirut, the Lebanese capital was placed under siege.

Fighting in the PLO and Syrian controlled city continued until August 1982, with IDF/AF air strikes being the principal weapon used against Arab forces in Beirut. A US-brokered agreement ending the fighting was finally signed by both sides on 11 August 1982, after which Syrian troops evacuated Beirut and rejoined the main force in Lebanon dug in just north of the Israeli occupied territory. Thousands of PLO fighters were duly deported from Beirut on 21 August 1982 and sent by boat to a new base that had been established in the Tunisian capital, Tunis.

The battle for Beirut had seen strike missions being flown round-the-clock by IDF/AF fighter-bombers, and in order to be better placed to protect these aircraft, the Spearhead Squadron sent a detachment to Ramat David air base in northern Israel.

Despite Syrian forces taking a pounding in Beirut, the seriously weakened SyAAF made no attempt to intercept IDF/AF jets, which were constantly over the city. However, this phase of the campaign did trigger a single air combat which saw the Spearhead Squadron claim its first kills.

On the morning of 24 June 1982, unit CO Yoel Feldsho and navigator Zvi Lipsitz were leading a two-ship CAP in F-15B Baz 979. Their wingman was Yiftach Shadmi, and the jets' call-sign was 'Hot'. Like both Feldsho and Lipsitz, Shadmi already had MiG kills to his credit.

At about 1000 hrs local time, the SyAAF scrambled two MiG-23MFs from Saikal air base, and these jets were joined a few minutes later by a pair of MiG-21s. This flurry of Syrian activity had been caused by the latest round of IDF/AF strikes on targets in the Beirut area.

The two MiG-23MFs were still climbing out over Baalbeck, in the Lebanon Valley, when the 'Hot' jets received their vector to engage. Although the SyAAF fighters were flying southwest in the general direction of Beirut, they were still a long way from the Lebanese capital. Indeed, the actual engagement would take place northwest of Rayak, which was within Syrian-controlled territory in Lebanon.

Like so many interceptions during the 1982 conflict, the first pilot to visually acquire the enemy jets was the wingman rather than the CAP leader. Therefore, in line with standard IDF/AF procedures, 'Hot 2' ran the engagement from then on, with 'Hot 1' now assuming the role of wingman. Feldsho subsequently acquired the targets when the Bazs were eight miles from the MiG-23MFs, and by then Shadmi was preparing to launch an AIM-7F – he fired his missile at the trailing jet from a distance of 2.4 miles in a perfect tail chase interception.

Unaware that 'Hot 2' had already engaged the MiG, Feldsho also fired a Python 3 at it from a range of just 800 metres and at an off-boresight angle of 45 degrees. The faster Python 3 hit first, causing the MiG-23MF to explode, and the AIM-7F flew into the fireball seconds later.

With one jet down, Lipsitz instructed his pilot to go after the lead SyAAF fighter. 'Hot 1' duly pulled the F-15B into a 10-12G (the precise level of G endured by the crew varies depending on who tells the story of the interception, and there are claims that Baz 979 remains structurally twisted to this day) banking turn in a manoeuvre that placed the jet 1.2 miles behind the MiG-23MF. Once again, an off-boresight angle of 45 degrees presented few problems to the Python 3 launched by Feldsho, and the missile scythed down the 'Flogger-G'. Two more MiGs had fallen victim to the Baz in an engagement that had lasted just over 30 seconds.

With hindsight, the 24 June 1982 clash was a portent of things to come for the IDF/AF fighter force. Both MiG-23MFs had been intercepted a long way from the hotspot of Beirut, and they did not pose an immediate threat against IDF/AF assets over the capital when intercepted by the F-15s. However, their destruction sent a warning to the SyAAF to keep away from Beirut, or suffer the consequences.

This warning was duly heeded by the MiG-21 and MiG-23 units, but with its troops besieged in the Lebanese capital, the Syrian government needed to keep an eye on IDF positions surrounding Beirut. It fell to high-flying MiG-25RBs to obtain photo-reconnaissance imagery of the area during a series of hazardous overflights that were made in the weeks after the ceasefire had 'ended' the war in June.

Baz pilots had already claimed two MiG-25 kills in 1981, although these had been achieved against the slightly slower MiG-25P fighter variant – the F-15 had yet to challenge the reconnaissance version of the 'Foxbat'. Soviet-manned MiG-25Rs had initially conducted overflights of Israel from bases in Egypt in 1971, and the F-15 had been specifically chosen for its ability to intercept these very aircraft. However, 11 years later, the IDF/AF had yet to down a photo-reconnaissance 'Foxbat-B'.

Several attempts were made by both Baz squadrons to intercept MiG-25Rs over Lebanon in June and July 1982, but these all resulted in failure. Indeed, unlike the other MiG types flown by the SyAAF, it appeared that the 'Foxbat-B' was untouchable. These failures galvanised the IDF/AF, which pooled resources and devised a combined operation aimed at stopping the overflights.

Flying at 70,000 ft and cruising at Mach 2.5, the MiG-25 was theoretically outside the engagement envelope of Israel's Improved HAWK SAM system. However, the IDF/AF came up with a two-tier attack plan that paired the Improved HAWK with an AIM-7F-equipped Baz. The SAM battery would be specially deployed on high ground in Lebanon so as to close the gap between the missile's engagement envelope that topped out at 55,000 ft and the MiG-25R's cruising altitude.

The 'Foxbat-B' was given the codename 'Nestling' by the IDF/AF, and an ambush was duly set in place for the aircraft. The first combined interception attempt was made on 12 August 1982 when a 'Nestling' was detected approaching Beirut. Once again this ended in failure, however, as the Improved HAWK battery failed to achieve a radar lock on the target. Subsequently, a technician manning the battery noticed that the Improved HAWK system was optimised to lock onto either fast and low or high and slow targets. For this reason alone, the weapon had failed to lock-up the MiG-25R on 12 August. The technician duly devised a simple override for the battery's guidance system that enabled the Improved HAWK to engage high and fast targets.

The battery was given another chance to prove its effectiveness on 31 August 1982, when the next 'Nestling' run was made over Beirut. This time a radar lock was achieved and two SAMs launched, and several minutes later they exploded close enough to the jet to damage it.

With his aircraft trailing black smoke, the MiG-25R pilot was forced to descend into the AIM-7F engagement envelope of two Spearhead Squadron's Bazs that had been scrambled specifically to intercept the crippled jet. Shaul Schwartz (in Baz 821) disposed of the MiG-25R with a solitary Sparrow AAM, thus giving him his third MiG kill. As an added bonus, the IDF retrieved the wreckage of the jet for close examination.

Fittingly, the credit for this kill was shared between the Improved HAWK battery and Schwartz.

## OPERATIONAL COMPETENCE

Up until 1982, the Baz had been a single-role air superiority jet, despite having the ability to carry bombs and hit a target with as much accuracy as the F-16. Indeed, the F-15 was a better bomber than previous generation IDF/AF strike aircraft such as the A-4, F-4 and Kfir.

However, there was little point in using the Baz as a 'mud mover' simply because the Israelis had plenty of other platforms that could bomb targets on the ground with reasonable accuracy. Conversely, the latter aircraft could not hope to emulate the F-15's proven mastery of the skies. Possessing only a single squadron of precious Bazs at that time, and with each one costing on average four times more than any other fast jet type in Israeli service, there was no way that the IDF/AF was going to risk losing these aircraft to AAA or SAMs while flying ground attack missions.

In the summer of 1982, two things happened that would eventually result in the Israelis clearing the Baz to conduct air strikes. Firstly, more F-15s arrived from the USA, thus allowing the IDF/AF to form a second squadron and still be able to adequately cover any future attrition. Secondly, the close-range threat on Israel's borders had been considerably reduced by the early 1980s following the signature of a peace treaty with Egypt, the inactivity of Jordan in relation to the wider Arab-Israeli conflict, the expulsion of the PLO from Lebanon, the IDF's occupation of southern Lebanon and the recent defeat of Syria.

Political leaders on both sides of the Arab-Israeli conflict now began re-evaluating the new diplomatic and military order in the Middle East. Arab air forces acknowledged that the F-15/F-16 partnership would dominate the skies of the region for years to come, and although the IADS concept had worked well in Egypt in 1969-70 and 1973, the effective SEAD campaign waged by the Israelis in Lebanon in June 1982 had negated this threat.

As a direct result of the IDF/AF's performance in the Lebanon War, Arab countries in the Middle East chose to invest heavily in the procurement of surface-to-surface missiles (SSMs) as a counterbalance to Israel's fourth generation fighter force, and its potent SEAD capabilities. The Syrians also added SA-5 very long-range SAM batteries to its IADS.

In response to the threat posed by SSMs, the Israeli military divided the region up into a series of strategic engagement circles. The first circle included Arab nations sharing a border with Israel, whilst the second circle covered countries (like Iraq and Libya) that did not share a border with Israel, but had a buffer nation in between. The third circle included hostile regimes with two buffer nations between their territory and Israel.

After 1982, the first engagement circle posed no real threat. However, countries with SSMs no longer needed a shared border to inflict damage on the Jewish state, as these could reach Israel if fired from the second or third engagement circles. The rise of the SSM forced the IDF/AF to reappraise its ability to conduct long-range operations, and as they grew in importance, so the Baz became more attractive as a strike aircraft.

A major boost to the F-15's long-range capability came with the delivery of the first IAI-converted Boeing 707 tanker to the IDF/AF in 1983. The introduction of Journal night-vision goggles at this time also greatly improved the jet's ability to hit targets in the hours of darkness.

With two Baz squadrons now in the frontline force, the IDF/AF decided to assign air supremacy missions exclusively to the Double Tail Squadron, and give the job of developing the F-15 into an air-to-ground platform to the Spearhead Squadron. Whilst the latter unit set about developing bombing mission profiles for the jet, its aircraft were modified to operate the GBU-15 electro-optical-guided glide bomb.

In a further enhancement of the F-15's mission capabilities, elsewhere at Tel Nof, a handful of Double Tail Squadron jets were also given a reconnaissance capability. These Bazs have been operated exclusively from a dedicated reconnaissance HAS on base since the mid 1980s.

## OPERATION *WOODEN LEG*

Thanks to the foresight shown by the IDF/AF that saw the Baz developed into a long-range strike aircraft following the Lebanon War, the Israeli

PGM capability was added to the Baz after the 1982 war in the shape of the GBU-15 electro-optical glide bomb. The weapon's data link pod was hung on the underfuselage centreline stores station and the two GBU-15s were mounted on the wing pylons. When flying a jet in this configuration, the pilot relied on the aircraft's 20 mm cannon and AIM-7 AAMs, attached to the CFT pack, for self-protection

government was able to authorise a strike on the PLO headquarters in Tunis in October 1985 following a terror attack on Israeli citizens far from home. The previous month, on 25 September, the PLO's Force 17 had attacked an Israeli yacht off the coast of Larnaca, Cyprus, killing the crew of three. This action would duly result in the IDF/AF carrying out its longest ever bombing mission.

Israel was a nation in crisis in 1985, with its economy on the brink of collapse following rampant inflation. The June 1982 war had yielded no diplomatic breakthrough with Israel's neighbours, or put a stop to the PLO terrorist threat, so on 14 January 1985 the Israeli government decided to withdraw from Lebanon. The pullout had been completed by June of that year, although a small IDF force remained to support the Christian militia in the buffer zone in southern Lebanon until May 2000.

Hundreds of Israeli soldiers had lost their lives in Lebanon between 1982 and 1985, yet no diplomatic solutions had been reached with neighbouring Arab countries as a result of this campaign. Even the PLO's deportation from Lebanon proved to be a hollow victory, as its guerilla war against Israel was continued by Shiite Muslim militia groups such as Amal Movement and Hezbollah, which were created following the war to fill the political vacuum left in the south of the country.

In a counter-terror operations conference held in 2005, a respected Israeli defence analyst summed up the situation facing the IDF post-1982 when he made the following analogy;

'A military force can defeat terror on the tennis court, only to find out

**Baz 708 *Merkevet Esh* (Chariot of Fire) is seen here performing pre-acceptance flight trials with the IDF/AF's first IAI-converted Boeing 707 tanker in late 1982. This aircraft entered service in 1983, and it immediately boosted the long-range effectiveness of the Baz fleet**

**The crew of Baz 970 flew as wingmen to the leader of the *Regel Etz* (*Wooden Leg*) mission to Tunis on 1 October 1985. The jet is seen here landing at Tel Nof two months prior to the long-range strike**

that the terrorists have already started playing basketball – an entirely new game on a new court.'

And this was the situation that Israel found itself in in 1985 following the Palestinian attack off Cyprus. The IDF had smashed the PLO's infrastructure in Lebanon, but the Palestinians had decided to open a new front far away from Israeli soil.

A massive retaliatory air strike was deemed by the Israeli government to be the only way the PLO could be deterred from this course of action, and the organisation's new HQ complex in Tunis, 1280 miles from Israel, was selected as the target.

Codenamed Operation *Wooden Leg*, the mission's planning and execution was entrusted to the Spearhead Squadron. At the heart of the attack would be six of the seven F-15B/Ds assigned to the unit, and they would be flown by the squadron's six GBU-15-qualified crews. These aircraft/crews would also be supported by other IDF/AF assets, including four Double Tail Squadron single-seat jets. Two single-seat Bazs would trail the two-seaters as Nos 7 and 8 all the way to Tunis, where they would drop unguided GP bombs. Two more Double Tail Squadron jets were part of the spare force for the mission, and they would fly with the primary strike aircraft until the critical in-flight refuelling point.

Once the jets had topped off their tanks, the eight F-15s would then press on with the mission and the two spare jets would return home. However, if one or two of the jets failed to take on sufficient fuel for the rest of the operation, or suffered a technical malfunction whilst on the tanker, the spare, or spares, would immediately take its place, leaving the faulty jet to head back to Israel.

As was the case with previous IDF/AF special operations, the *Wooden Leg* aircrew were the best in their field when it came to using PGMs. Sticking with tradition, the formation's still officially unidentified senior officer flew in the Baz that occupied the No 4 position, as had been the case in 1981 when fellow Mirage IIIC ace Yiftach Spector led the Osirak raid in a brief break from his job as CO of Ramat David air base. Seven of the aircrew involved were already MiG killers, while an eighth participant would join this prestigious group the following month.

The Israeli government authorised the strike on 26 September 1985 and the aircrew involved flew a complex training mission the following day in order to practise the in-flight refuelling drill and PGM delivery

The *Regel Etz* jets overfly Tel Nof in close formation at noon on 1 October 1985, having just returned from bombing the PLO HQ complex in Tunis. Of the three two-seaters visible in this rare photograph Baz 450 was the only one that failed to deliver its GBU-15 on target – Baz 280 and Baz 455 were both credited with direct hits. Note that the national markings and unit emblems were painted out prior to the mission being flown

A Baz navigator examines the steering mechanism in the tail of the GBU-15 affixed to the left wing stores pylon of his Baz prior to departing Tel Nof for Tunis on 1 October 1985

Baz 450, armed with a full complement of air-to-air missiles (four AIM-7s and four AIM-9s) and a GBU-15 data-link pod on the fuselage centreline station, prepares to taxi from the Last Chance point at Tel Nof on 1 October 1985. It returned to base six hours later, having failed to drop its solitary GBU-15 (attached to the left wing pylon) on target due to a technical malfunction with the jet's bomb delivery system

aspects of the operation. With preparations complete, on the morning of 1 October the Baz crews headed to their jets at the start of the IDF/AF's longest ever bombing mission.

The ten F-15 strike aircraft took off at 0800 hrs local time, with the No 5 jet pressing on to the tanker despite one of its two multi-function displays refusing to work. An hour into the flight, the Bazs rendezvoused with two Boeing 707 tankers, and the in-flight refuelling phase of the mission was successfully accomplished. With each aircraft now laden down with 13.5 tons of fuel, the F-15s pressed on to Tunis, whilst the two air spares headed home.

After one final INS update, the formation split into two flights of four in trail, with a four-minute separation interval. A few minutes later, another technical malfunction struck the No 3 jet when the aircraft's bomb delivery system went off line whilst the PGMs were being given a final check time by the crews. Since each Baz had its own aim point within the PLO HQ compound, there was no back-up available that could bomb No 3's target. The crews quickly discussed target reallocation, but it was decided to keep things as they were, for individual crews were intimately acquainted with their respective targets.

For the GBU-15 to be effective, its engagement envelope was dependent on a clear line of sight between the target and the data link equipment carried in the retreating bomber – clouds and smoke greatly affected the navigator's ability to guide the bomb. The maximum drop altitude and range for the PGM was 40,000 ft and 24 miles, respectively. As the bomb glided down towards the target, the pilot broke away from the area while the navigator continued to guide the PGM to its aim point using a television camera image transmitted from the bomb to the Baz via a data link pod. This picture was the 'uplink' in the system, while the steering input to the bomb from the Baz's navigator was the 'downlink'.

As the bombers began to approach the Tunisian coast, Baz crews were dismayed to see plenty of cloud in the sky near the target area. And it was only when they got closer to Tunis itself that they were relieved to see that the target area was cloud-free, which meant that the PGM attack could indeed go ahead.

Once within range, the first three Baz bombers released their ordnance – following a wait of 90 seconds, three direct hits were seen. It was now the second wave's turn to attack, with Nos 5 and 6 dropping their PGMs. Only the weapon released by the first jet scored a direct hit, however, for No 6's bomb missed the target.

Having expended his GBU-15, the mission leader now joined up with the final pair of F-15s (which were not armed with PGMs) on their bombing run so that his navigator could photograph the smoking ruins of the PLO HQ complex. No 8 acquired his target and released the six 500-lb Mk 82 bombs carried on the jet's underbelly vertical ejector rack. However, thick smoke over the target precluded the pilot of the No 7 jet from visually identifying his aim point, so he and the formation leader circled Tunis once more, before returning for a successful bombing run that was made from a different direction.

Israel immediately announced that the attack had been a complete success. The PLO's HQ compound was in ruins, up to 75 people (of which around 60 were PLO members, some reportedly from Force 17) had been killed and dozens more were injured.

Leaving a shell-shocked Tunis behind them, the F-15 crews headed east – each jet was still carrying ten tons of fuel. Their flight home to Tel Nof was made that much easier after they rendezvoused with a command & control Boeing 707 that had also been involved in the mission. With the latter jet acting as a mother-ship, the F-15s all landed safely back at base at 1400 hrs local time, thus ending the six-hour operation. This mission had lasted almost twice as long as the Osirak raid of 1981.

## FINAL BAZ KILL TO DATE

Seven weeks after *Wooden Leg*, the Baz was credited with its final aerial kills in Israeli service to date. The IDF/AF had continued to fly reconnaissance missions over Lebanon in an effort to keep an eye on Syrian positions north and east of Beirut, and although the SyAAF had monitored these sorties, it had not opposed them to date.

Typically, the IDF/AF would send three flights of aircraft on a reconnaissance mission. A formation of four F-15s would flush out any SyAAF fighters that were waiting to ambush the RF-4E, which was given additional cover by four F-16s in trail.

When Syrian fighters were scrambled, they usually attempted to intercept the Israeli jets head-on. The latter would respond by turning into the MiGs, and both sides then attempted to 'paint' the other with their respective fire control radars. SyAAF and IDF/AF jets would typically get to within 10-15 miles of each other before the Syrian command & control centre ordered the pilots to break off the engagement and return to base. Typically, Israeli GCU also refused to give the escorting Baz and Netz fighters clearance to chase the Syrian MiGs down as they fled east.

On 19 November 1985, in a break from the norm, four F-16s were in the lead formation and a similar number of F-15s provided the rearguard. The latter jets were

Spearhead Squadron commander Avner Naveh alights from Baz 840 *Commando* on 19 November 1985, having just participated in the Baz's final aerial engagement to date. He was credited with 1.5 kills following this clash, thus taking his score to 6.5 victories overall. He was now the world's leading F-15 ace. Naveh had achieved his tally in just three engagements – two kills in his first aerial combat on 24 September 1979, three kills in his clash on 10 June 1982 and 1.5 kills on 19 November 1985. Naveh's mount on the latter occasion was already marked up with four SyAAF roundels prior to him downing the MiG-23s, thus providing yet another case of incorrectly applied victory symbols! This aircraft had been previously used by Benny Zinker to destroy a MiG-23 on 10 June 1982 and by Yiftach Shadmi to down a MiG-21 the following day ordered by IDF command & control to engage two SyAAF MiG-23s that had been detected. However, by the time the F-15s were cleared to attack, they had turned away from the Syrian aircraft after the Arab fighters had ended their standard 'drill' approach at a distance of 15 miles from the Israeli jets.

Spearhead Squadron CO Avner Naveh (in Baz 840), along with wingmen Yuval Ben-Dor and Ofer Paz (in F-15D Baz 957), quickly changed direction and headed due east in pursuit of the fleeing enemy jets. Their initial attempts at a BVR engagement failed, for both AIM-7Fs that were fired homed into the ground clutter – a common fault with the weapon. Now much closer to the fleeing MiG-23s, the Baz crews switched to the Python 3 option, and this time made short work of the 'Flogger-Gs'. Naveh had boosted his tally to 6.5 victories, having shared credit for the second MiG with his wingmen.

## SUPERIORITY AND DETERRENCE

The F-15's ability to perform both BVR and WVR interceptions was enhanced from 1986 when the Elbit DASH Helmet-Mounted Display (HMD) was introduced, initially only to those flying two-seat Bazs. The HMD considerably improved the aircrews' situational awareness by presenting HUD data directly onto the helmet's visor, thus giving the pilot and navigator freedom to look outside the jet, rather than having to look through the fixed HUD – HMD proved crucial when an off-boresight engagement was being fought. 'Look and shoot' now replaced 'point and shoot'.

Now a fully matured multi-role platform equipped with the latest technologies, the Baz celebrated its tenth anniversary in IDF/AF service in late 1986. Six months later, the first examples of a new fourth generation fighter capable of rivalling the F-15 for control of the skies in the Middle East finally began to reach Arab air forces. The MiG-29 'Fulcrum' that began entering service in Iraq and Syria indeed posed a threat to the Baz hegemony, but its capabilities were more of a match for the lightweight F-16 rather than the heavyweight F-15.

Having secured air superiority for the IDF/AF, the issue of whether the Baz played a part in deterring a potential enemy from acting aggressively towards Israel was less easy to quantify. The jet had indeed achieved the level of deterrence envisioned for it by the IDF/AF when the F-15 was procured at great expense in the mid 1970s, but did its mastery of the skies in the region have any lasting effect on Israel's enemies?

The Baz was indeed a formidable war machine, but it would prove to be totally irrelevant in the next round of hostilities fought between Arabs and Israelis – namely the Palestinian uprising in the Gaza Strip and the West Bank that erupted in December 1987, and which still continues to this day. IDF troops trained to engage the enemy in a war zone now faced

*Below and bottom*
Pilot Ziv Nadivi (right) and navigator Yehoar Gal (left) pose beside Baz 957 soon after landing the one-winged jet at Ramon air base following an eventful DACT mission in May 1983. During the course of a 1-v-1 engagement with an A-4, the F-15 struck the Skyhawk and lost almost its entire right wing. In an amazing feat of airmanship, the Baz crew managed to land the wingless jet at Ramon, which had the closest runway long enough for a high speed recovery. The jet was transported from Ramon to the AMU at Tel Nof on 13 May 1983, where it was repaired. With four kills already to its credit, the fighter claimed a half-share in the destruction of one of two MiG-23s that were shot down on 19 November 1985

young Palestinians armed with semi-automatic rifles and rocket-propelled grenades in the crowded and narrow streets of cities, towns and villages.

The Baz force's operational activity was also at an ebb in the late 1980s, with three precious F-15s being lost in accidents and Spearhead Squadron commander Amos Yadlin being removed from office after almost shooting down his wingman on 1 April 1988.

Yadlin and his wingman Shai Gilad had returned from an operational mission in fully armed jets that still had plenty of fuel in their tanks. As was the custom at the time, both pilots opted to practise a 1-v-1 air combat scenario rather than dump fuel in order to get the jets down to their landing weights. Failing to follow the appropriate safety checks that would have disarmed his missiles, Yadlin pressed the trigger when he got on the tail of Gilad and, to his horror, a live missile shot off a launch rail. Luckily for his wingman, the F-15 is one of the world's most survivable fast jets, and the Baz withstood the impact.

Just as Ronen Shapira had landed his one-engined, battle-damaged jet in 1982 and Ziv Nadivi had somehow got his one-winged F-15 down in 1983 following a mid-air collision during an ACM sortie, Gilad brought his Baz back to base. Yadlin accepted full responsibility for the incident and prematurely ended his term as squadron CO.

Four months later, on 15 August 1988, Yadlin's counterpart in the Double Tail Squadron also ended his tenure prematurely, but in far more tragic circumstances. Ram Caller was killed when his jet collided with an F-15 flown by Ehud Falk during an air combat training session – the latter pilot also died.

The loss of these jets, together with the crash of an F-15B in April 1987 and Guy Golan's accident in September 1979, reduced the active Baz fleet to 46 jets. In an effort to bring the force back up to the optimum level of 50 aircraft, and to further enhance the long-range multi-role capability of the Double Tail and Spearhead Squadrons, Israel secured the purchase of five F-15Ds for a staggering $265 million in 1988.

By the time delivery of the five Multi-Service Improvement Program Baz 4s (Project *Peace Fox IV*) commenced in May 1992, the F-15 force had once again been involved in a major crisis in the Middle East which further highlighted the jet's air superiority/deterrence value.

**Top and above**
Baz 223 *Ha Nammer Ha Meofef* (The Flying Tiger) was the first of two F-15Ds delivered as part of Project *Peace Fox III*. Having served as the lead bomber in the *Regel Etz* mission to Tunis on 1 October 1985, the jet was lost in a fatal accident on 1 April 1987. The top photograph was taken less than two months prior to its demise, while the bottom shot shows the burned out wreckage of the fighter following its low speed, flat spin, crash. Pilot Yiftach Mor was killed in the accident, but navigator Ofer Paz became the first person to successfully eject from a Baz

71

# RAAM INTRODUCTION AND BAZ UPGRADE

Having revealed its ability to strike targets well beyond Israel's borders, the Baz force unwittingly played a major part in the 1991 campaign to free Kuwait following its seizure by Iraq. President Saddam Hussein had identified Israel as the weak point in the United Nations' Coalition of countries that had been pulled together under the leadership of the USA in an effort to drive Iraqi troops out of Kuwait. Although Israel was never actually part of the Coalition, the Iraqi leader knew that if he could draw the Jewish nation into the fight, it would transform the conflict from being an Arab war into an Arab-Israeli war. Should the latter transpire, the Arab countries committed to the Coalition against Iraq would almost certainly withdraw their support.

In an effort to keep Israel distanced from the conflict, the UN asked it to temporarily relinquish its long-standing policy of forceful retaliation in response to Arab aggression. With Iraq being so far away from Israel, any kind of strike following attacks on Jewish soil would involve the Baz force, and it was these very aircraft that the Coalition was now working so hard to keep within Israeli airspace through ongoing diplomatic efforts.

The Coalition's force build-up in the region was geared towards 15 January 1991, when the ultimatum to Iraq to retreat from Kuwait was due to expire. The IDF/AF stepped up its state of readiness as this date approached, and the Baz squadrons felt the impact of this heightened state of alert. Maintenance schedules were either rushed or relaxed so that a maximum number of jets would be available on the 15th, while EP and reserve aircrews were instructed to report to their squadrons.

The Baz force was tasked with flying continuous CAP missions on a 24-hour basis, seven days a week, in preparation for a possible pre-emptive strike by the Iraqis on Israel.

Baz aircrew and groundcrew also acclimatised themselves with nuclear-biological-chemical (NBC) suits, flying and working in this cumbersome equipment. Intelligence reports had indicated that

**Baz 654 (F-15A 76-1505)** *Horikan* **(Hurricane) prepares to launch on a CAP mission on 15 January 1991 – just 48 hours prior to the start of the second Gulf War. The aircraft is configured in the standard CAP missile fit for the period, being armed with four AIM-7F SARH and four Python 3 IR AAMs. This head-on view reveals the 'cranked' geometry of the** *Magrefa* **(Rake) pylon installation that had to be developed to allow the aircraft to accommodate Python 3 missiles on either side of the external fuel tanks. The smaller AIM-9L utilised a simpler pylon that sat perpendicular to the fuel tanks. Missile carriage grew even more complicated for the Baz force when CFTs were attached to the fuselage, armourers then being restricted to Python 3s on the outer fuel tank launcher rails only, with AIM-9Ls having to be fitted on the inner rails**

Iraq possessed a substantial arsenal of chemical weapons that included both aerial bombs and warheads for SSMs. And as the Iraqis had employed these weapons against Iran and Kurdish insurgents, Israel could not rule out the possibility of such an attack.

The most challenging scenario potentially facing Baz pilots was an attack from Iraqi Su-24 bombers in the wake of an SSM attack. In an effort to negate this threat, the IDF/AF planned to augment the airborne CAP during SSM strikes. However, verifying whether or not an SSM was carrying chemical weapons took some time, so Baz aircrew and groundcrew had to scramble jets whilst wearing full NBC gear just in case they were indeed operating in such an environment.

With the Double Tail Squadron leading the CAP effort, the Spearhead Squadron was tasked with mounting retaliation strikes against Iraqi aggression. And the latter unit came close to flying just such a mission on 19 January 1991 in the wake of an SSM attack on Israel at 0200 hrs on that date. Aircrew had been fully briefed on their targets, and were strapped into their jets, when the cancel order was received at Tel Nof.

At the eleventh hour, the Israeli government agreed to obey the UN Coalition request to refrain from launching Baz strikes in retaliation for the attack. In an effort to protect Israel from further SSMs, the US government rushed PAC-1 (Patriot Anti-Tactical missile Capability-1) batteries to Israel, while the Coalition increased the number of 'Scud Hunting' sorties it was flying in western Iraq. In the longer term, Israeli restraint in the face of extreme provocation would benefit the Baz force.

Iraq eventually launched 40 Al-Hussein SSMs against Israel between 19 January and 25 February 1991, these weapons being a longer range, locally built, development of the Soviet R-17E Scud B SSM. Hundreds of

A Spearhead Squadron maintainer clears the pilot of Baz 541 *Hook* to taxi out from the HAS in early 1991. Again, this F-15 is seen in CAP configuration, with four AIM-7s and four Python 3 AAMs. Note also the AN/ALQ-131 EW pod on the centreline pylon in place of a third external tank. Unlike the Raam, which was equipped with a fully built-in active-passive Elisra EW suit from the outset, the Baz had, and still has, an internally-mounted passive EW system, but has to rely on podded EW equipment. Baz 541 was the fifth *Peace Fox III* F-15C delivered to the IDF/AF

Wearing full NBC suits, Double Tail Squadron maintainers perform the Last Chance drill around Baz 663 in January 1991

apartments were damaged, more than 200 people were injured, one person died and others lost their lives as a result of heart attacks and suffocation in their NBC masks during the SSM attacks. Ultimately, however, no chemical weapons were employed and the Su-24s did not follow up the missile strikes.

Had an SSM caused a large loss of life, hit a site of religious significance or been equipped with a chemical warhead, the Israeli government would have almost certainly reassessed its policy of restraint. Luckily for Israel, and the UN Coalition, none of these scenarios eventuated.

The long CAP missions of January-February 1991 were flown 24 hours a day in all weather conditions during one of the worst winters in Israeli history, these flights proving once again that Beni Peled was right to emphasise the importance of adequate instrument flying training for would-be F-15 pilots.

By early February the threat of an Iraqi air strike had diminished, although sporadic SSM attacks continued throughout the month. Four of the six SSM strikes on Israel up to 26 January 1991 had seen missiles fired in salvos of four to eight, with the remaining two attacks involving a single SSM fired at night. In subsequent strikes between 28 January and 25 February, an average of two SSMs were launched per night.

The Baz force's reaction to the diminished threat changed accordingly, with round-the-clock CAPs ending on 12 February. By then the IDF/AF's Year 1991 Term 1 Baz Conversion Course, which had been postponed so as to allow the Baz force to concentrate on its preparations for the defence of Israel, had also resumed. Such courses were run by the Spearhead Squadron, and within days of Term 1 resuming, the F-15 force suffered its fifth fatal accident when conversion course student Israel Ornan lost control of Baz 821 on 10 February 1991 and crashed.

## REWARD

In the aftermath of the second Gulf War, Coalition forces revealed how they had struggled to find Scud and Al-Hussein transporter-erector launchers in the vast wastes of Iraq's western desert. Such an admission acted as a spur for SSM purchasing programmes initiated by other Arab countries in the region, forcing Israel to invest heavily in both defensive and offensive missile countermeasures systems.

Amongst the host of anti-SSM concepts that surfaced in the early 1990s was a proposal to have Baz CAPs that were flying over suspected missile sites intercept the weapons just seconds after they had launched. A preliminary investigation carried out by the IDF/AF proved that such intercepts were technically feasible, although the aircraft's radar and weapon system would have had to have been modified to allow the Baz to engage a target that was vertically accelerating.

Israel and Jordan signed a peace treaty on 25 October 1994, after which the Israeli government granted Jordan permission to use an air corridor through its airspace for airliners flying to and from Amman. Three months prior to the signing of the peace treaty, Israeli Prime Minister Yitzhak Rabin and King Hussein of Jordan met in Washington on 25 July 1994. In the wake of this meeting, Israel granted King Hussein special permission to overfly its territory for the first time. King Hussein himself duly flew a Royal Jordanian Airlines L-1011 TriStar from Amman to Israel, making this low-level pass over Tel Aviv in the process. The airliner was escorted by fully armed Spearhead Squadron jets Baz 575 *Maadim* (Mars) and Baz 965 *Tsipur Ha Esh* (The Fire Bird) throughout the L-1011's time in Israeli airspace

The Rafael Python 4 entered IDF/AF service in 1994, thus revolutionising WVR air combat. While work on the Python 3 had started prior to the F-15's arrival in Israel, the Python 4 had been designed with the Baz in mind from the word go. The weapon was built to be fully compatible with Elbit Systems' Display And Sight Helmet, which entered IDF/AF service in 1986. This lethal combination ushered in the 'look-and-launch' WVR engagement era, replacing 'point-and-launch' AAMs in the process. Rafael commenced an export sales campaign with the Python 4 in October 1996, when it released this photograph of Baz 678 armed with four of the AAMs

The tails of five ex-USAF Baz 5s (394, 312, 387, 361 and 332) protrude from the former Mirage IIIC readiness sunshelters at Tel Nof. Most of the Baz 5 single-seat jets were assigned to the Double Tail Squadron, although a few became Spearheads, including Baz 361. The final Baz 5 F-15A to be issued to the latter unit was Baz 317 *Lavi* (Lion)

*Peace Fox V* Baz 111 *Hod Ha Khanit* (The Spear Head) was the first of the ex-USAF F-15Bs to be allocated to the Spearhead Squadron, hence its name. The first three *Peace Fox V* F-15Bs had been delivered to the Double Tail Squadron, leaving the remaining trio to be issued to the Spearhead Squadron. After two of the latter squadron's F-15Bs were lost in accidents in 1997-98, the unit was left with just a solitary B-model jet (Baz 111). The Double Tail Squadron duly transferred one of its three Baz 5 two-seaters (Baz 109) to the Spearheads in 1998

More conventional thinking resulted in the modification of two-seat F-15B/Ds so that they could launch Rafael Popeye air-to-surface missiles. This weapon, which had previously been used only by IDF/AF F-4Es, was a 1360-kg electro-optical guided missile with a range of more than 90 kilometres when launched from high-altitude. Popeye significantly boosted the Baz's stand-off attack capability, as the jet had previously relied solely on the GBU-15 glide bomb for precision strikes.

Spearhead Squadron commander Amos Yadlin had initially forwarded a request to have the Baz made Popeye-capable in 1987-88, and aircraft received an accelerated modification following the 1991 conflict. Shortly

after the Popeye joined the Baz's arsenal, another Rafael missile was introduced which further improved the aircraft's air-to-air WVR engagement performance. Production examples of the Python 4 were added to the Baz's weaponry suite in 1994, this missile being recognised at the time as the world's best WVR AAM.

As previously mentioned, Israeli F-15 units benefited greatly from the second Gulf War, as not only were their jets upgraded with additional weapons and associated systems, they also received additional airframes as part of *Peace Fox V*. The latter project rewarded Israel for its restraint in the face of Iraqi SSM attacks with the delivery of 25 Excessive Defence Article F-15A/Bs drawn from USAF stocks – 19 single-seat and six two-seat jets would be delivered to Israel from October 1991 onwards.

Modifying these aircraft so that they were comparable with Israeli F-15s was a major task that covered the removal of all USAF equipment that was not IDF/AF compliant. Baz avionics, communications equipment and EW systems were fitted in their place, and the jets were made Python, Popeye and GBU-15 capable.

The six F-15Bs were modified first, in light of the IDF/AF's urgent need to augment its long-range PGM Baz force. The first two-seat Baz 5 to be overhauled and issued to the Double Tail Squadron emerged from the Aircraft Maintenance Unit (AMU) facility at Tel Nof in 1993.

A few months after this aircraft had been delivered, the Baz force was again committed to combat operations. Hostilities between Israel and Hezbollah along the Israeli-Lebanese border had intensified during early 1993, and on 25 July the IDF launched Operation *Accountability*.

Numerous Hezbollah targets were bombed and shelled in southern Lebanon, with the IDF/AF flying 979 air-to-ground sorties during seven days of fighting. Baz aircrew flew both CAP sorties and air strikes, with the latter missions being the first time that Israeli F-15s had dropped bombs in anger since the Tunis Raid in October 1985. These sorties also marked the first time that the Baz had participated in close-range Israeli Homeland Security bombing strikes.

## DIPLOMACY DIVIDEND

By modifying the Baz so that it could drop PGMs, the IDF/AF had been able to rapidly field a long-range strike aircraft in response to the threat facing Israel from enemies further afield post the Lebanon War in 1982. However, there were too few Bazs available to allow them to conduct the type of long-range, round-the-clock, operations now being asked of the IDF/AF in the fight against the growing SSM threat in the Middle East.

Baz 109 *Kalia Ha Kesef* (The Silver Bolt) was the first *Peace Fox V* Baz 5 jet to be modified by the AMU to IDF/AF standard, the jet being rolled out of the Tel Nof workshop in 1993 and delivered to the Double Tail Squadron. The AMU modified the jet's avionics, communication equipment and VTR so as to enable the 'new' jets to operate alongside those aircraft already in frontline service. All of the IDF/AF airframes, bar the four FSD jets, were actually younger than these ex-USAF *Peace Fox V* F-15s. Seen at a damp Tel Nof in 2003, this aircraft bears full Spearhead Squadron markings

In an effort to reduce the burden now placed on the F-15 squadrons, the Israelis duly issued a requirement in 1993 for a long-range, multi-role combat aircraft that would ultimately be purchased in sufficient numbers to equip two frontline squadrons. The Lockheed Martin F-16C/D was initially viewed as the obvious answer to this requirement in light of the IDF/AF's vast experience with the aircraft over the past 13 years, with McDonnell Douglas' F/A-18C/D being seen as a rank outsider. The two jets were duly evaluated in Israel in late 1993, but were both declared to be inadequate for the task due to their modest range.

The IDF/AF publicly stated shortly after the evaluation that the aircraft that best complied with its operational requirements for this mission was the F-15E Strike Eagle, which had been in service with the USAF since 1988, and was not yet cleared for export.

Although Israeli restraint in the 1991 conflict had resulted in the delivery of second-hand F-15A/Bs, it had not prompted an offer from the US government for Strike Eagles. However, the same kinds of diplomacy that had enabled Israel to purchase the F-15A/B in the 1970s once again worked in the IDF/AF's favour to give it access to the Strike Eagle, which is arguably the best tactical strike fighter of its generation.

In the wake of the Oslo Accords, signed by Israel and the PLO in August 1993 in an effort to end the conflict between the two sides, US President Bill Clinton promised Israeli Prime Minister Yitzhak Rabin that he would ensure that the IDF maintained a qualitative edge over the armed forces of its neighbours. The supply of military hardware again proved to be all the incentive Israel needed to proceed with the diplomatic process. And with the US government agreeing to sell a less sophisticated version of the Strike Eagle to Saudi Arabia as the F-15S, the Israelis were now cleared to purchase the F-15E.

The IDF/AF was eager to make the most of this opportunity, but securing the necessary funding to acquire two squadrons' worth of Strike Eagles was no easy matter. Although prohibitively expensive, the F-15E easily met all the mission parameters laid down by the IDF/AF in its 1993 long-range, multi-role combat aircraft requirement. The Strike Eagle had proven in the 1991 Gulf War that it had the ability to operate at night and in poor weather conditions on long-range missions. The jet was capable of advanced weapons integration, both with US and Israeli munitions, and it could perform the air-to-air mission just as well as the F-15C/D.

Although the Strike Eagle easily met all of the IDF/AF's operational requirements, its price tag was causing the Israeli government problems. The latter had allocated a budget of $1.8 billion to cover the purchase of a new strike aircraft, and these funds would have bought 55 F-16C/Ds or 45 F/A-18C/Ds. However, only 28 F-15Es could be purchased for the same price, which was not enough to equip two squadrons.

Faced with having to field a smaller force of F-15Es than it wanted to, the IDF/AF looked at possibly buying ten F-15Es and a squadron of either F-16C/Ds or F/A-18C/Ds in what was effectively a quantity over quality purchase. Senior officers duly hoped that the acquisition of at least ten F-15Es would lead to follow-on buys in subsequent years, thus slowly increasing the IDF/AF's Strike Eagle force to squadron-strength.

Once again, the US government's special relationship with Israel came to the fore and solved this fiscal conundrum when it agreed to supply 50 surplus USAF F-16A/Bs to the IDF/AF. By offering these aircraft to the Israelis, the Americans had ensured that the number of fourth generation fighters in service with the IDF/AF would not have to be reduced in order to fund the purchase of a squadron of F-15Is.

Despite the Israelis announcing the selection of the Strike Eagle as their new long-range strike aircraft, its huge price tag continued to motivate Lockheed Martin as it strove to sell the IDF/AF an aircraft that was just as capable of performing this demanding mission, but at a fraction of the price per jet. Realising that it had no direct rival for the F-15E at the time because the F-16ES (Enhanced Strategic) proposal, which featured a Fighting Falcon equipped with CFT packs, was still little more than a 'paper' aircraft, Lockheed Martin came up with a surprising offer.

Instead of purchasing a single squadron of new F-15Is and receiving two squadrons of F-16A/Bs, Lockheed Martin offered Israel the opportunity to buy two squadrons of new F-16C/Ds and a squadron of ex-USAF F-111Fs, all for considerably less than $1.8 billion.

The IDF/AF carefully studied this new proposal, as the F-15E was, of course, the successor to the F-111 in USAF service. As part of this evaluation, IDF/AF commander Hertzel Bodinger visited RAF Lakenheath, where the USAF's 48th Wing was in the process of transitioning from F-111Fs to F-15Es. He and his staff also consulted both the USAF and the Royal Australian Air Force in an effort to discover what the jet was like to fly and maintain on a daily basis.

The IDF/AF concluded that the F-111 was a superb aircraft to fly in all weather, but that it lacked a true all-weather attack capability. Unlike the F-15E, its had no effective air-to-air capability whatsoever. The sheer size of the maintenance effort that had to be expended on the aircraft in order to keep them serviceable was also noted, with old technology power-plants, analogue computers and vintage systems being rated a nightmare to work on.

Israeli Prime Minister and Minister of Defence Yitzhak Rabin approved the F-15I purchase plan in January 1994, and a $2 billion letter of acceptance covering the purchase of 21 aircraft was signed on 12 May 1994.

Invited guests examine the Spearhead Squadron's Baz 137 *Hetz Ha Kesef* (The Silver Arrow) during an IDF/AF Open Day in June 1995 (below). Two months later, on 10 August 1995, the unit lost F-15B Baz 965 when it suffered a massive bird strike. Pilot Ronen Lev and navigator Yaron Vayonte both perished in the crash, so the squadron renamed Baz 137 *Yaron Ronen* (bottom) in their honour. In a cruel twist of fate, the latter jet was lost in an accident on 19 January 1997 during a training flight over Kibbutz Revivim, in the Negev Desert. The unnamed aircrew lost control of the jet after it entered a spin from which they could not recover. As per standard IDF/AF procedures, the Baz crew ejected as the jet descended below an altitude of 6000 ft. Both men survived, making this the one and only wholly successful ejection in Baz history to date. The *Peace Fox V* F-15B (USAF 74-0137) hit the ground only 200 metres from the Kibbutz

The only *Peace Fox V* F-15B not to take its IDF/AF tail number from the last three digits of its USAF serial was Baz 142 *Keren Or* (Ray of Light), which was originally 73-0112. This Spearhead Squadron jet was lost in a fatal accident on 1 March 1998, when the squadron's Junior Deputy Commander Uri Kolton and navigator Uri Manor crashed during a strike training mission. The cloud base that day over the target area near Nablus was 4000 ft – less than 150 ft above the minimum safe height altitude for a nearby mountain peak (3084 ft), atop which was a 300-ft high antenna. The mountain and antenna combined then had an additional minimum safety altitude of 500 ft immediately above them. Despite the cloud base, the crew of Baz 142 commenced their attack run on the target from a height of 6000 ft, and had briefed to commence their recovery at 3000 ft, with a minimum hard deck height of just 500 ft. At some point in their attack run the jet entered cloud and hit the antenna atop the mountain and crashed

Boeing test pilot Joe Felock and USAF Weapon Systems Operator Maj Rick Junkin performed the first flight of the F-15I (in 94-0286) from St Louis, Missouri, on 12 September 1997. A formal roll out of the aircraft followed on 6 November 1997. The jet was subsequently rigged up with test instrumentation and assigned to the USAF's Flight Test Center (FTC) at Edwards AFB, where it remained until ferried to Israel in September 1999 and issued to the IDF/AF's FTC as Raam 201

The IDF/AF was so keen to purchase the F-15I that it deferred a planned buy of Sikorsky UH-60 Black Hawk assault helicopters so that more money could be injected into the project's coffers – a budget increased from $1.8 to $2 billion overall. The F-15I deal also included an option for an additional four jets, and this was duly taken up with the US Department of Defense on 22 December 1995 when a follow-on $253 million contract was signed.

In order to emphasise the difference between the earlier F-15A/B/C/D Baz and the new F-15I, the IDF/AF named the latter jet Raam (Thunder), pronounced Ra-am. The purchase price also covered the provision of a two-seat flight and systems trainer constructed by Lockheed Martin which was designed to serve the whole IDF/AF F-15 community from Baz to Raam. This equipment was eventually activated in 2003 as part of a new simulation 'farm' at Hatzor air base.

As with previous fourth generation aircraft to enter service with the IDF/AF, the Raam's Israeli systems can be found in three key areas – command & control, EW and weaponry. The jet relies on the Elta secure communication system (the F-15I has no fewer than four radios, covering short range inter-formation to very long-range communication) and the Rafael data link, whilst its EW requirements are serviced by Elisra's SPS-3000 active and passive system. The pilot and navigator wear Elbit HMDs, and Rafael has configured the jet to accept a wide range of locally-produced weapons, as well as equipment supplied from the USA.

Finally, additional Israeli avionics such as the RADA data collection and transfer system, as well as structural components including IAI-built CFT assemblies, have also been added to the aircraft as part of an offset

deal with Strike Eagle manufacturer Boeing.

The first F-15I made its maiden flight on 12 September 1997, and an official roll-out ceremony was held at St Louis on 6 November that same year. The first two aircraft were delivered to Israel in January 1998, and deliveries were completed in September 1999. The last F-15I to enter squadron service was in fact the very first Raam built (aircraft 201), this jet having been temporarily fitted with instrumentation and additional wiring to serve with the IDF/AF's Flight Test Centre.

## HAMMERS' LEGACY

As the IDF/AF's first F-15 unit, the Double Tail Squadron had been formed from scratch in 1976, while the Spearhead Squadron was activated in 1982 following 33 years of dormancy. It had previously existed for less than a year as a Curtiss C-46 Commando transport unit.

In sharp contrast to the less than heroic heritage of the two Baz squadrons, the Raam unit's legacy was a glorious one. The Hammers Squadron had originally been activated in July 1948 as only the fourth unit to be formed in the fledgling IDF/AF. It had acquired its title through the operation of three Boeing B-17 Flying Fortress bombers during the 1948-49 Israeli Independence War and the 1956 Sinai campaign, after which the unit was inactivated until 1969, when the Hammers became the IDF/AF's second F-4 squadron.

Flying from Ramat David air base throughout its time as a B-17 unit and for most of its second incarnation with the F-4, the Hammers had relocated to Hatzerim in 1991 and then been deactivated three years later so as to give the squadron time to prepare for the Raam's introduction.

The first two F-15Is arrived in Israel on 19 January 1998, and the Hammers were declared operational on 1 January 1999 following the delivery of 16 Raams. The unit flew its first operational sortie, over southern Lebanon, ten days later, and the Hammers remained active in this area until the final Israeli withdrawal from the country in May 2000.

One of the more noteworthy missions flown by the Raam during this period occurred on 24 June 1999, when the CO of the Hammers Squadron destroyed bridges over the Litani and Awali rivers during the course of a single night mission. This sortie graphically demonstrated the F-15I's endurance, load-carrying capacity (four 2000-lb LGBs, expended in pairs per bridge) and advanced targeting sensors, which made such an accurate attack possible despite the partially cloudy night sky.

## RAAM WEAPONS

Based at Hatzerim air base in the Negev Desert, the Hammers Squadron compound includes a Flying Flight building, a Technical Flight

**Raam deliveries commenced on 19 January 1998, when the first two aircraft landed at Hatzerim air base, in the Negev Desert. F-15I 94-0287 (top) arrived first, followed minutes later by 94-0288 (above). The final Raam was delivered to the IDF/AF in September of the following year, and the chances of additional F-15s entering Israeli service currently seem remote. Prior to purchasing the F-16I, the IDF/AF had considered buying more Raams in order to allow the formation of a second squadron to offset delays with the procurement of the JSF. And with South Korea's F-15K purchase keeping the Strike Eagle production line open, there is always a chance that the IDF/AF might buy more F-15Is towards the end of this decade, should the JSF service entry date continue to slip to the right**

Building, HAS complexes and secured weapons storage facilities. The Flying Flight consists of all the aircrew, as well as a small number of related specialists who man the navigation, intelligence and operations cells. The Technical Flight is responsible for the preparation and maintenance of the aircraft, while a small Adjutant Flight handles the squadron's administration.

The Hammers Squadron is a multi-role unit, and as such its aircrew have to be proficient in all aspects of the air-to-ground and air-to-air missions. When conducting the latter, the unit employs three types of weapon – 20 mm cannon, WVR AAMs and BVR AAMs

The 20 mm M61AI Vulcan cannon is still regarded as a valid weapon, and although its technology has not evolved much over the years, the introduction of an improved gunsight and more aerodynamic ammunition has ensured better accuracy at longer ranges. Both AIM-9L and Python 4 IR AAMs can be fitted to the jet, although aircrew prefer the latter weapon thanks to its 90 degrees off-boresight launch capability. This effectively means that the pilot simply has to look at his foe once he is in missile range to achieve target lock-on, as all the firing solution information is being presented to him through HMD data projection in front of his right eye.

As a result of the AAM's immense off-boresight launch capability, the pilot has to take care to avoid any kind of 'friendly fire' scenario. Indeed, the Python 4 has an automatic failsafe system fitted into it that prevents it from being launched if a friendly fighter is in the target's immediate vicinity. This restriction is not as limiting as it may at first seem, however, since the Python 4's homing head only has a 2.5-degree field-of-view (FOV). Therefore, the weapon will not home on any target that falls outside this FOV, no matter how off-boresight the AAM is launched.

For BVR engagements, the Raam is armed with either AIM-7M or AIM-120 AMRAAM active radar-homing missiles. The former has a range of up to 20 miles, although this is effectively halved when fired in a head-on engagement scenario, as the interceptor and the target will have rapidly closed on one another while the weapon is in flight. The AIM-120 was unique to the Raam until the introduction of the first Baz AUP (Avionics Upgrade Programme) in 1999 and the F-16I six years later.

Once launched, the AIM-120's trajectory is divided into three phases. In the first, silent, phase, the AIM-120 receives updated target data from the launch platform. The missile can be used as a 'fire and forget' weapon, but the supplementary information from the launch jet increases the probability of a kill.

In the second phase, the AIM-120's radar is activated in intermediate pulse repetition frequency mode, which changes to multiple pulse repetition frequency during the final phase of the AAM's trajectory. The Raam, or any other AIM-120 launch platform for that matter, does not have to follow the AAM's trajectory, or continuously 'paint' the target with its radar, as is the case with the AIM-7.

The F-15I's air-to-ground arsenal includes general purpose 'dumb' bombs, cluster bomb units, laser-guided bombs, electro-optical guided bombes, JDAM GPS-guided bombs and the Popeye ASM.

The most recent weapon cleared for use by the F-15I is the GBU-28 'bunker-busting' bomb. The US Defense Security Cooperation Agency

notified the US Congress on 26 April 2005 of the planned sale of 100 GBU-28s to Israel, noting that the IDF/AF would 'employ these weapons from their F-15 aircraft'. Media reports at the time highlighted the fact that the GBU-28 could potentially be used in an Osirak-style attack on Iranian nuclear installations, although journalists chose to ignore the threat much closer to Israel – deep tunnels in the Gaza Strip used by the militant group Hamas during the low-intensity conflict that has been fought between Israel and the Palestinians since 2000.

Supporting the Raam's comprehensive weapons fit are two LANTIRN pods – the AN/AAQ-13 navigation and AN/AAQ-14 targeting pods. The AN/AAQ-13's terrain-following radar (TFR) system is linked to the jet's automatic pilot, while the pod's FLIR imagery is projected onto the pilot's HUD. Low-level AN/AAQ-13 training missions are restricted to a minimum altitude of 300 ft, although the pod can fly the F-15I down to 100 ft if necessary. Flight control inputs from the pod are affected by the jet's altitude, and the lower it flies the aircraft, the more gentle its instructions for manoeuvring become due to the TFR's FOV limitations at low level. Integration of the Rafael Litening targeting and navigation pod with the F-15I has been ongoing since 2003.

During nocturnal operations, Raam aircrew use Journal NVGs attached to their lighter nighttime helmets – F-15I pilots and navigators have two tailor-made helmets that they wear, with the daytime helmet being HMD-compatible and the nighttime helmet NVG-compatible. In order to avoid any light returns that might degrade aircrew vision during nocturnal NVG operations, the Raam's cockpit interior is painted black.

The F-15I can carry almost 16 tons of fuel when equipped with external tanks, and this is typically reduced to seven tons when loaded with ordnance. Most multi-role combat aircraft must trade fuel in order to lift a significant war load, but the Raam can still carry a respectable four tons of bombs and missiles even when laden down with close to 16 tons of fuel. The jet's range is theoretically unlimited thanks to in-flight refuelling and autonomous life support equipment such as the onboard oxygen generation system, which has replaced time-limited oxygen bottles featured in previous generations of combat aircraft.

Post-mission debriefing is aided by the aircraft's video tape recorder system that simultaneously records four of the multi-function display (MFD) units in the two cockpits. There are no less than 16 computers

Raam 209 and Raam 238 prepare to depart Hatzerim on a Popeye ASM training sortie. Both jets are in an asymmetric load configuration similar to that employed by the F-15B/Ds sent on the 1985 Tunis raid, only then the latter jets were armed with GBU-15s rather than Popeyes, as the ASM only entered IDF/AF service in 1986. The locally-developed Popeye has been the weapon of choice for the IDF/AF's F-4, Baz and Raam heavy strike force for the past 20 years. With electro-optical terminal guidance, the missile's TV camera footage is uplinked to the jet via a data link pod (seen here just behind and below both ASMs). The navigator in turn uses a small console-mounted joy stick to guide the missile to its target via steering inputs relayed to the weapon through the downlink

A highly-coveted Raam aircrew patch

and nine display screens in the Raam, the pilot having an up front control (UFC) screen and three MFD units, one of which is in colour. The navigator also has a UFC screen, as well as four MFD units, two of which are in colour. There are 27 options that can be displayed on any of the seven MFDs, although the most 'popular' screens are the radar picture, the moving map (or satellite image) display, on which locked-on targets are superimposed, and the EW screen.

Much of the information shown on these screens is derived from the AN/APG-70 radar fitted into the aircraft, this system providing a coverage range in air-to-air mode of 95 to 125 miles. Its resolution in ground-mapping mode is also hugely impressive.

Raam aircrew feel that their jet is a multi-role combat aircraft that has been created without compromise. It therefore has a huge advantage over other so-called multi-role jets that have had to trade performance in a certain mission to achieve acceptable capability in another. The only trade off with the F-15I is the huge amount of effort that Hammers Squadron personnel have to put in in order to remain competent in the wide variety of missions that they are tasked with performing.

## BAZ AUP

Updating the Baz has been an IDF/AF priority since the mid-1980s, with initial studies focusing on two options – the USAF's Multi-Stage Improvement Program (MSIP) and the IAI's Baz 2000 proposal. The two fundamental elements of MSIP were the introduction of the

IDF/AF maintainers state that the F-15 is considerably more robust than the lightweight F-16. This is just as well for the pilot of Baz 552 *Akev* (Buzzard), who endured a minor off-runway excursion at Tel Nof in the sixth *Peace Fox III* F-15C (83-0059) in December 1995

The IDF/AF celebrated the Golden Jubilee of the state of Israel between April 1998 and April 1999, and during this period it adorned a number of its aircraft with special Jubilee logos that were applied either with the help of airbrushed stencilling or via self-adhesive decals. Both Double Tail jets seen in this photograph (MiG-25 killer Baz 673 and Baz 714) sport the larger airbrushed artwork on the outer surfaces of their vertical stabilisers. The latter aircraft was the fifth and final *Peace Fox IV* F-15D (90-0279) delivered to the IDF/AF, and it was modified with test instrumentation for reassignment to the FTC shortly after this photograph was taken at Tel Nof

AN/APG-70 radar, which featured track while scan (TWS) mode that gave the pilot the ability to conduct multi-target engagements as had been available to F-14 aircrew since the jet's service entry in 1972, and integration of the AIM-120. The IDF/AF was already acquainted with MSIP, as all Baz 4 jets had been delivered with TWS fitted as standard.

The Baz 2000 proposal saw the avionics developed by IAI for its Lavi multi-role combat aircraft project (cancelled by the Israeli government on 30 August 1987) integrated into the F-15.

Tight budgets forced the IDF/AF to continue with the incremental introduction of new technologies into the Baz when a comprehensive upgrade was postponed by the Israeli government. The latter felt that the F-15 force could still retain aerial supremacy in the region without having to resort to an expensive update of the jet's systems.

After almost a decade of upgrade postponements, the actual catalyst for the launch of the Baz AUP came with the purchase of the Raam in 1994. The IDF/AF convinced the Israeli government to integrate elements of the F-15I's modern avionics into the proven F-15A/B/C/D airframes that were still equipped with avionics installed in the 1970s.

The principal element of the Baz AUP was the transformation of the cockpit instrumentation and displays from analogue to digital. As a result of this change, a common cockpit standard was at last achieved across the previously diverse Baz fleet. The integration of new weapons such as the AIM-120, improved avionics and upgraded EW and communication systems were also included as part of the AUP.

Elbit Systems' colour MFDs dominate the Baz AUP cockpit, whilst an F-15I-type Hands On Throttle And Stick (HOTAS) grip enhances crew ergonomics. The central and weapon system computers have also been replaced, as have all the command & control systems and the 1970s' vintage electrical harnesses. Finally, a GPS system and a data link have been installed too. The new avionics require more cooling air, especially in the single-seat jets, so all AUP aircraft feature a new air conditioning system.

There was no space available within the airframe of the Baz for the new avionics, which effectively meant that these systems could not be installed by simply replacing old black boxes with new ones. Engineers had to totally redesign the jet's internal architecture, but without resorting to expensive structural modifications. For example, replacement electrical harnesses were routed via existing holes in the structure so as to avoid having to drill new holes that would require complicated stress analysis.

With the airframes stripped down, engineers discovered that there were minor internal differences between jets that externally looked to be identical. For example, Baz 2 jets had a longer shelf in one of their avionics bays than Baz 3 jets, so the latter aircrafts' shorter shelves had to be replaced with the formers' longer shelves in order to house new equipment.

As part of the AUP for the F-15B/D, the jet's rear cockpit was redesigned with two colour MFDs and HOTAS technology to allow the back-seater (still termed 'navigator' in IDF/AF terminology) to operate both offensive and defensive systems.

Initially, all jets were upgraded to Block A standard, with new computers, new displays, additional hard points and modified existing

Photographed in April 2001, Baz 678 displayed an early iteration of the AUP tail art that was applied exclusively to the outer surface of the jet's left vertical stabiliser. The definitive version of this artwork (see the photograph opposite) was considerably larger, and painted on the outer surfaces of both vertical stabilisers

hard points. HOTAS was introduced on Block B standard jets after exhaustive inputs from squadron pilots had been analysed at the avionics integration laboratory.

The Baz AUP was launched in 1994 with an allocated budget of $40 million from US Foreign Military Funding and $12.5 million for local expenditure in Israel. The first major contract was awarded in August 1995 to IAI Lahav Division and Elbit Systems for the joint development and construction of an avionics integration laboratory to validate the Baz AUP concept. Two months later, RADA was awarded a contract to supply data transfer equipment and a debriefing system. US-based Baz AUP contractors were Boeing (which was to redesign all existing weapon hard points and add two more), Hughes (radar improvements), Honeywell and Loral.

Overall, the AUP was run by the IDF/AF as an in-house project, and its primary aim was to create a Baz that boasted avionics performance that was identical or better than that achievable with the Raam.

The actual upgrade work was entrusted to AMU engineers at Tel Nof, and their CO, Shmuel Cozy, remarked in January 2006;

'The IDF/AF directly pays for any changes it makes to the specification in a contracted project. In an in-house project like the AUP, there is a strong temptation to add capabilities, but this in turn causes the upgrading process to last longer. The end product may be better than the original specification, but this improvement comes at a considerable cost both in terms of time and money. Despite the complexity of the project, the AMU managed to keep the Baz AUP on schedule. I believe that without this upgrade, the Baz would have been irrelevant to the modern battlefield.'

The AMU covered the upgrading of the entire active IDF/AF F-15A/B/C/D fleet except for the first four FSD airframes that had been delivered to Israel in December 1976. The first A, B, C or D airframe to be upgraded was treated as a 'prototype' for that model, and the first AUP aircraft to be rolled out was two-seat Baz 706 in November 1998.

A single F-15 consumed between 7000 and 9000 working hours when going through the AUP, and as the project progressed, the AMU began scheduling upgrades so that they coincided with a jet's periodic depot

Three Baz 4 AUP jets (706, 715 and 733) departed Israel on 28 August 2003 and headed to Poland to attend the Polish Air Force's 85th anniversary airshow, which was staged over the weekend of 30-31 August. On their way home, on 4 September, the three-ship formation performed a flypast over Auschwitz-Birkenau. Located near the Polish village of Oswiecim, Auschwitz-Birkenau was the largest of the 2000 Nazi concentration and extermination camps. More than a million Jews were murdered in Auschwitz-Birkenau, which was equipped with four gas chambers that could each kill up to 6000 people per day. The flypast coincided with an IDF delegation visit to the site, led by IDF/AF Head of Air Group Iddo Nechushtan

maintenance overhaul. This meant that a staggering 18,000 working hours would be spent on the aircraft over six to seven months. Shmuel Cozy remarked 'It was not a simple serial upgrade project – we treated each and every jet differently on an airframe by airframe basis, as invariably Baz "X" was not the same internally as Baz "Y"'.

The Baz AUP was completed with the rollout of Baz 280 on 28 November 2005 – exactly seven years after the first upgraded jet had been returned to frontline service. And although the entire fleet of active F-15s has just completed a comprehensive avionics upgrade that has allowed an ageing warrior to remain a formidable foe in combat, ongoing improvements continue today. Indeed, the Baz force will become JDAM-compatible in the near future, a fourth generation display and sight helmet will soon be available, new EW equipment is scheduled for installation (as are new chaff and flare dispensers) and a radar altimeter has been procured for fitment.

Such investment will see the Baz remain a viable weapons platform with the IDF/AF for many years to come.

**Further improvements to the Baz force have continued in the wake of the AUP. In late 2005, the FTC's test instrumented Baz 714 *Nesher Ha Barzel* (The Golden Vulture) commenced periodic depot maintenance at the nearby AMU, so the center was loaned Spearhead Squadron Baz 701 *Shual Hayesh* (The Fire Fox) for datalink trials. In this early 2006 view, the jet is equipped with an Elta active EW pod as it sits inside an FTC sunshelter between flights**

**Double Tail Squadron Baz 113 *Zeev Boded* (Lone Wolf) taxies in at Tel Nof on a hot spring day in 2005. An ex-USAF *Peace Fox V* jet (73-0113), the Baz has already been upgraded, as indicated by the AUP tail art**

# APPENDICES

## APPENDIX I

### BAZ KILLS

| DATE | SQUADRON | AIRCREW | BAZ | KILL | WEAPON | NOTES |
|------|----------|---------|-----|------|--------|-------|
| 27 June 1979 | Double Tail | Melnik, Moshe | 663 | MiG-21 | Python 3 | |
| 27 June 1979 | Double Tail | Feldsho, Yoel | 704 | MiG-21 | AIM-7F | |
| 27 June 1979 | Double Tail | Peled, Yoram | 672 | MiG-21 | AIM-9G | |
| 27 June 1979 | Double Tail | Ben-Eliyahu, Eitan | 689 | MiG-21 | cannon | |
| 24 September 1979 | Double Tail | Naveh, Avner | 695 | MiG-21 | Python 3 | |
| 24 September 1979 | Double Tail | Naveh, Avner | 695 | MiG-21 | cannon | |
| 24 September 1979 | Double Tail | Rosenthal, Dedi | 676 | MiG-21 | AIM-7F | |
| 24 September 1979 | Double Tail | Shafir, Relik | 692 | MiG-21 | AIM-9G | |
| 24 August 1980 | Double Tail | Margalit, Ilan | 696 | MiG-21 | AIM-7F | |
| 31 December 1980 | Double Tail | Rachmilevic, Yair | 646 | MiG-21 | AIM-9G | |
| 31 December 1980 | Double Tail | Stern, Yoav | 695 | MiG-21 | Python 3 | shared victory with an F-4E aircrew |
| 13 February 1981 | Double Tail | Zinker, Benny | 672 | MiG-25 | AIM-7F | |
| 29 July 1981 | Double Tail | Simon, Shaul | 673 | MiG-25 | AIM-7F | |
| 7 June 1982 | Double Tail | Lapidot, Offer | 658 | MiG-23 | Python 3 | |
| 8 June 1982 | Double Tail | Schwartz, Shaul and Reuven Solan | 957 | MiG-21 | AIM-7F | |
| 8 June 1982 | Double Tail | Hoffman, Yoram | 686 | MiG-21 | AIM-7F | |
| 8 June 1982 | Double Tail | Simon, Shaul | 818 | MiG-23 | AIM-7F | shared victory with Rosenthal |
| 8 June 1982 | Double Tail | Rosenthal, Dedi | 832 | MiG-23 | AIM-7F | shared victory with Simon |
| 9 June 1982 | Double Tail | Shapira, Ronen | 684 | MiG-23 | AIM-7F | |
| 9 June 1982 | Double Tail | Rapaport, Gil | 658 | MiG-23 | AIM-7F | |
| 9 June 1982 | Double Tail | Melnik, Moshe | 802 | MiG-23 | AIM-7F | |
| 9 June 1982 | Double Tail | Maor, Avi | 646 | MiG-23 | Python 3 | |
| 9 June 1982 | Double Tail | Melnik, Moshe | 802 | MiG-21 | Python 3 | |
| 9 June 1982 | Double Tail | Maor, Avi | 646 | MiG-21 | cannon | |
| 9 June 1982 | Double Tail | - | - | MiG-23 | No Weapon | Squadron Kill |
| 9 June 1982 | Double Tail | - | - | MiG-23 | No Weapon | Squadron Kill |
| 9 June 1982 | Double Tail | Peled, Yoram | 684 | MiG-21 | Python 3 | |
| 9 June 1982 | Double Tail | Shapira, Ronen | 686 | MiG-21 | Python 3 | |
| 9 June 1982 | Double Tail | Hampel, Oran | 695 | MiG-21 | AIM-7F | |
| 10 June 1982 | Double Tail | Naveh, Avner and Michael Cohen | 957 | MiG-23 | AIM-7F | |
| 10 June 1982 | Double Tail | Naveh, Avner and Michael Cohen | 957 | MiG-23 | Python 3 | |
| 10 June 1982 | Double Tail | Naveh, Avner and Michael Cohen | 957 | MiG-21 | Python 3 | |
| 10 June 1982 | Double Tail | Nadivi, Ziv | 848 | Gazelle | Python 3 | |
| 10 June 1982 | Double Tail | Zinker, Benny | 840 | MiG-23 | Python 3 | |
| 10 June 1982 | Double Tail | Rapaport, Gil | 828 | MiG-23 | Python 3 | |
| 10 June 1982 | Double Tail | Knaani, Noam | 802 | MiG-23 | Python 3 | |
| 10 June 1982 | Double Tail | Knaani, Noam | 802 | MiG-23 | Python 3 | |
| 10 June 1982 | Double Tail | Schwartz, Shaul and Uzi Shapira | 708 | MiG-21 | Python 3 | |
| 10 June 1982 | Double Tail | Hoffman, Yoram | 848 | MiG-21 | cannon | |
| 10 June 1982 | Double Tail | Lev, Mickey | 955 | MiG-21 | Python 3 | |
| 10 June 1982 | Double Tail | Peled, Yoram and Zvi Lipsitz | 979 | MiG-21 | Python 3 | |
| 10 June 1982 | Double Tail | Shadmi, Yiftach | 667 | MiG-21 | Python 3 | |
| 11 June 1982 | Double Tail | Peled, Yoram | 678 | MiG-23 | AIM-7F | |
| 11 June 1982 | Double Tail | Peled, Yoram | 678 | MiG-23 | AIM-7F | |
| 11 June 1982 | Double Tail | Shadmi, Yiftach | 840 | MiG-21 | Python 3 | |
| 11 June 1982 | Double Tail | Simon, Shaul and Amir Hodorov | 704 | MiG-21 | Python 3 | |
| 11 June 1982 | Double Tail | Lapidot, Offer | 646 | MiG-21 | Python 3 | |
| 24 June 1982 | Spearhead | Feldsho, Yoel and Zvi Lipsitz | 979 | MiG-23 | Python 3 | |
| 24 June 1982 | Spearhead | Feldsho, Yoel and Zvi Lipsitz | 979 | MiG-23 | Python 3 | |
| 31 August 1982 | Spearhead | Schwartz, Shaul | 821 | MiG-25 | AIM-7F | shared victory with SAM HAWK battery |
| 19 November 1985 | Spearhead | Naveh, Avner | 840 | MiG-23 | Python 3 | |
| 19 November 1985 | Spearhead | Naveh, Avner | 840 | MiG-23 | Python 3 | shared victory with Ben-Dor and Paz |
| 19 November 1985 | Spearhead | Ben-Dor, Yuval and Ofer Paz | 957 | MiG-23 | Python 3 | shared victory with Naveh |

# APPENDIX 2

## BAZ AIR-TO-AIR EXCHANGE RATIOS AND KILL WEAPONS

| Timeframe | Kills-to-Losses | Kill Weapons |
|---|---|---|
| June 1979 to July 1981 | 12.5-to-0 | 5 AIM-7, 2.5 Python 3, 3 AIM-9 and 2 cannon |
| June 1982 Lebanon War | 33-to-0 | 10 AIM-7, 19 Python 3, 2 cannon and 2 No Weapon |
| June 1982 to November 1985 | 4.5-to-0 | 0.5 AIM-7 and 4 Python 3 |

# APPENDIX 3

## BAZ LOSSES

| DATE | SQUADRON | AIRCREW | BAZ | CAUSE | NOTES |
|---|---|---|---|---|---|
| 29 September 1979 | Double Tail | Golan, Guy | 676 | landing accident | pilot killed |
| 1 April 1987 | Spearhead | Mor, Yiftach and Ofer Paz | 223 | spin | pilot killed, navigator ejected |
| 15 August 1988 | Double Tail | Caller, Ram | 684 | collision | pilot killed |
| 15 August 1988 | Double Tail | Falk, Ehud | 672 | collision | pilot killed |
| 10 February 1991 | Spearhead | Ornan, Israel | 821 | unknown | pilot killed |
| 10 August 1995 | Spearhead | Lev, Ronen and Yaron Vayonte | 965 | bird strike | pilot and navigator killed |
| 19 January 1997 | Spearhead | names withheld | 137 | spin | pilot and navigator ejected |
| 1 March 1998 | Spearhead | Kolton, Uri and Uri Manor | 142 | flew into antenna | pilot and navigator killed |

# COLOUR PLATES

## 1
### F-15A Baz 620, Double Tail Squadron, Tel Nof, July 1977
Baz 620 (FSD F-15A 72-0116) was the very first F-15 to arrive in Israel. Like the USAF, the IDF/AF retained the Eagle's standard Compass Ghost scheme of FS 36320 Dark Ghost Gray and FS 36375 Light Ghost Gray, with the tail numbers applied in black. The only markings visible on the jets aside from the smaller warning stencils were the IDF/AF's Star of David Shield beneath the cockpit and on the wings (both uppersurfaces and undersides) and the Double Tail Squadron emblem on the outer surfaces of the vertical stabilisers. The four FSD airframes were delivered in December 1976 with shorter and thicker aerodynamic slender bodies atop their left vertical stabilisers as was standard on all USAF Eagles – they housed radar warning receiver antennas that were not fitted to Israeli jets. The remaining *Peace Fox* F-15s were delivered with longer and thinner aerodynamic slender bodies, and these were retrofitted to the four FSD airframes in the early 1980s.

## 2
### F-15B Baz 704, Double Tail Squadron, Tel Nof, May 1978
Baz 704 was the first of two *Peace Fox* F-15Bs delivered to the IDF/AF, and Yoel Feldsho duly used the jet to claim his second kill on 27 June 1979 – his first dated back to 7 October 1973, when he claimed an Egyptian MiG-21 whilst flying an F-4E during the October 1973 Yom Kippur War. Feldsho was later credited with two more kills whilst serving as the Spearhead Squadron's first CO in June 1982. Baz 704 added a single kill to its tally when Shaul Simon and Amir Hodorov used it to down a MiG-21 on 11 June 1982. By then the aircraft carried the name *Hetz Mi Keshet* (Arrow From Bow). In the mid-1980s the jet's tail number's prefix digit '7' was replaced by a '4'.

## 3
### F-15A Baz 673 *Ha Oketz*, Double Tail Squadron, Tel Nof, 1981
Soon after Moshe Melnik succeeded Benny Zinker as the third CO of the Double Tail Squadron in May 1981, he ordered that all Bazs be adorned with individual names in Hebrew font on the left side of the jet's forward fuselage. Melnik stated that single-seat Bazs would be given single-word names, while the two-seaters would boast two-word titles. The first four Baz FSD airframes were duly named after the first four jet types operated by the IDF/AF, but there was no single theme to link the names chosen for the remaining *Peace Fox* jets. Six of these were allocated names preceded by *Ha*, which is the Hebrew equivalent of (text continues on page 92)

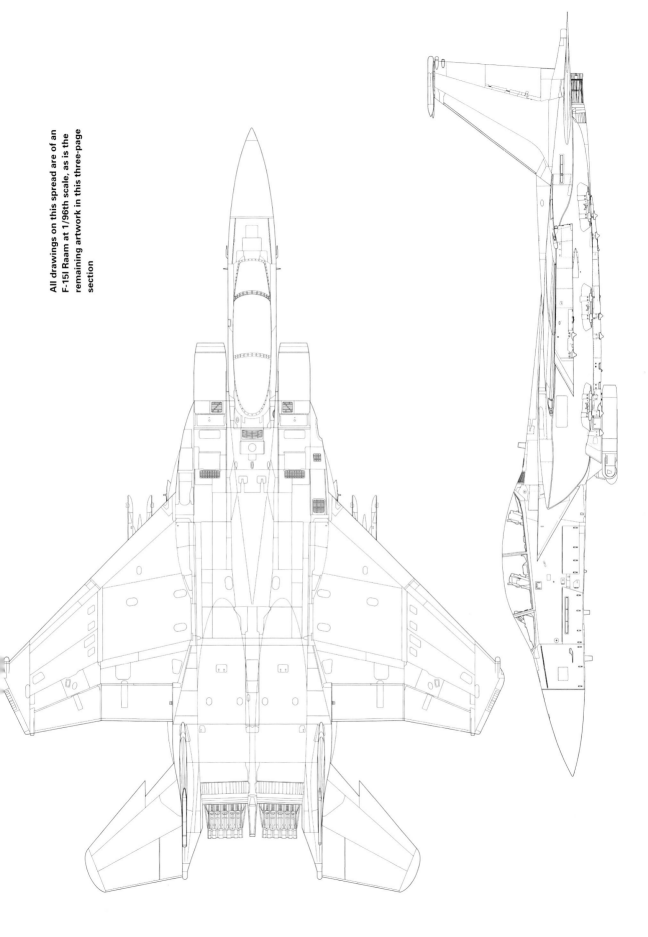

All drawings on this spread are of an F-15I Raam at 1/96th scale, as is the remaining artwork in this three-page section

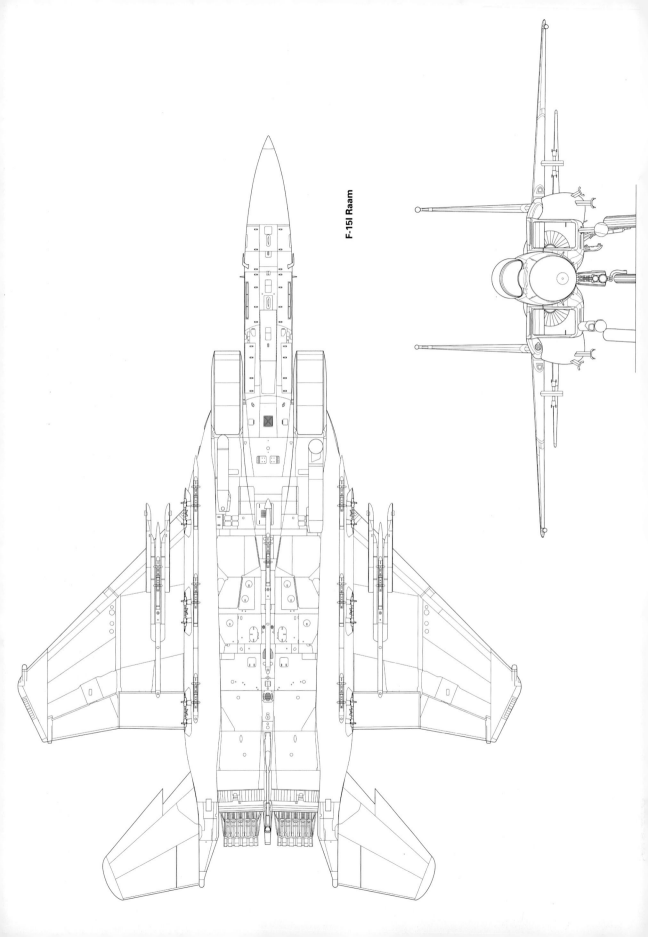

F-15I Raam

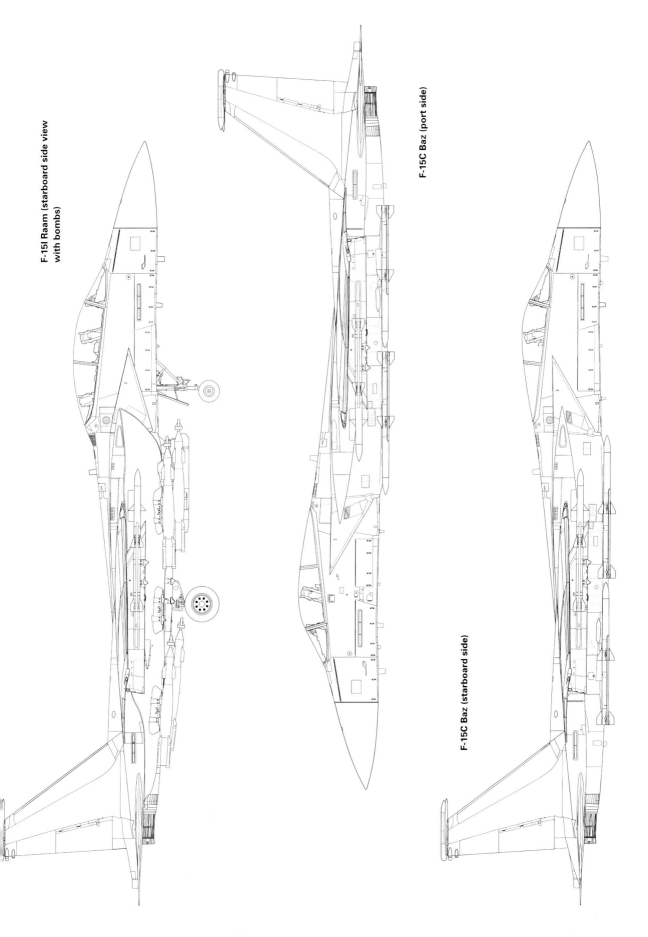

F-15I Raam (starboard side view with bombs)

F-15C Baz (port side)

F-15C Baz (starboard side)

'the'. Baz 673 *Ha Oketz* (The Sting) was one of six two-seaters in Melnik's squadron at the time, and the jet claimed its solitary kill (a MiG-25) whilst being flown solo by Shaul Simon on 29 July 1981.

## 4
### F-15A Baz 684 *Ha Arpad*, Double Tail Squadron, Tel Nof, 1982
*Peace Fox* jet Baz 684, which was named *Ha Arpad* (The Vampire) in 1981, claimed two AAM kills on 9 June 1982. Ronen Shapira used an AIM-7F to down a MiG-23 during a morning CAP and Yoram Peled destroyed a MiG-21 with a Python 3 whilst on an afternoon patrol. Although the F-15 was not a 'flying missile battery', as the IDF/AF labelled the F-14 in 1974 after evaluating the Navy interceptor, it was well equipped for medium-range BVR and short-range WVR engagements thanks to its four AIM-7Fs and four Python 3s. The latter had entered IDF/AF service in 1978 to augment the AIM-9G, and it was in turn slowly replaced by the next-generation Python 4 from 1994 onwards. During this same period, the AIM-7F was augmented by the improved AIM-7M/P, until progressively replaced by the vastly superior AIM-120 from 1996.

## 5
### F-15C Baz 802 *Panther*, Spearhead Squadron, Tel Nof, 1983
For more than 30 years the IDF/AF's Security Department censored all photographs that showed jets carrying unit badges. However, from the mid-1980s onwards, a new enlightened approach came into effect whereby badges and unit markings were applied to numerous aircraft, and especially those chosen to be put on public display during Israeli Independence Day and the IDF/AF Day. Baz 802 *Panther* was just such an aircraft, being the Spearhead Squadron's air day favourite for much of the early 1980s. The first of nine *Peace Fox II* F-15Cs, this aircraft was adorned with four kill markings following its exploits in June 1982. Over the years, six Bazs have been adorned with four kill markings at one time or another. Only three of these jets are entitled to wear these SyAAF victory emblems, however, and Baz 802 is one of them. Depicted here in its pre-1984 scheme, the aircraft has not yet had its tail numbers applied to both sides of its forward fuselage – a procedure that was adopted in the wake of a fatal F-4E accident on 22 January 1984.

## 6
### F-15D Baz 455 *Roach Pratzim*, Spearhead Squadron, Tel Nof, October 1985
The second of six *Peace Fox II* F-15Ds, this aircraft was initially given the tail serial 955 and named *Roach Pratzim* (Stormy Wind). The jet was one of the three *Peace Fox II* F-15Ds credited with an aerial kill during the June 1982 war, Mickey Lev (flying alone in the fighter) claiming a MiG-21 on the 10th while the jet was still assigned to the Double Tail Squadron. By the time of its participation in Operation *Regel Etz* (*Wooden Leg*) on 1 October

1985, *Roach Pratzim* had become the Spearhead Squadron's Baz 455. It was one of the four F-15Ds that successfully delivered their GBU-15s against targets in the the PLO HQ complex in Tunis – these aircraft had their national and unit markings obscured prior to conducting this mission. In 2002, a GBU-15 delivery 'kill' marking was applied to the jet alongside its SyAAF kill roundel.

## 7
### F-15A Baz 695 *Ha Kochav*, Double Tail Squadron, Tel Nof, July 1989
Baz 695 *Ha Kochav* (The Star) was marked up with four victory symbols and adorned with a stylised eagle's head in 1989 when it became the Double Tail Squadron's display jet. This aircraft currently has a clone on display in the IDF/AF Museum in the form of Baz 5 73-0098. An ex-USAF jet supplied to Israel in the early 1990s, the fighter never actually entered active service with the IDF/AF. Instead, it was used as a spares source until 1999, when the AMU refurbished the airframe and painted it up as Baz 695 for museum display. One of the first F-15As delivered to the USAF, 73-0098 served with the 58th Tactical Fighter Training Wing at Luke AFB from September 1975, and it is possible that the jet was flown by some of the ten Israeli pilots that were involved in the first two Baz conversion courses that were hosted by this unit in 1976-77.

## 8
### F-15C Baz 519 *Eitan*, Spearhead Squadron, Tel Nof, 1990
The second of nine *Peace Fox III* F-15Cs, this aircraft was the first of its type to be named in memory of a deceased Baz community pilot. Baz 519 *Eitan* is depicted here in typical long-range air-to-air configuration for this period, the aircraft boasting a CFT pack and three external fuel tanks, as well as two AIM-7s attached to the CFT and two Python 3s on the outer semi-*Magrefa* (Rake) missile pylons. Spearhead Squadron aircraft still lacked the unit's distinctive red wedges on the inner surfaces of their vertical stabilisers at this stage, with these not being applied until 1991.

## 9
### F-15A Baz 646 *Raam*, Double Tail Squadron, Tel Nof, January 1991
Double Tail Squadron pilots were keen to add a fifth kill marking to Baz 646's tally of four victories during the second Gulf War in early 1991. However, the Iraqis never attempted a manned air strike against Israel, and the IDF/AF's SSM retaliation operation was scrapped in line with the Israeli government's policy of restraint. Nevertheless, Baz pilots flew round-the-clock CAP missions in F-15s configured with three external fuel tanks and a full array of air-to-air weaponry – four AIM-7s and four Python 3s. Despite being a highly successful airframe, Baz 646 Raam (*Thunder*) was not chosen to undertake the Baz AUP because of its age – the fighter was the last of the four F-15A FSD airframes (72-0120) supplied to the IDF/AF in December 1976.

## 10
### F-15C Baz 840 *Commando*, Spearhead Squadron, Tel Nof, May 1992

Seven of the nine *Peace Fox II* F-15Cs were named after predators, with the two exceptions being Baz 832 *Ha Shishi Be Yuni* (The Sixth Of June), which was the only single-seat Baz to depart from Moshe Melnik's dictum of single word names, and Baz 840 *Commando*. Although the latter jet was named after the ungainly Curtiss C-46 transport, examples of which served with the IDF/AF in its early days, Baz 840 has enjoyed a highly successful two decades in frontline service. For many years the fighter was marked up with six kill symbols in a single long row forward of the cockpit, although this total bore no relation to its actual victory tally of two MiG-23s and a MiG-21 destroyed and one MiG-23 shared destroyed. The jet's final public appearance with six kill symbols came in 2001, and since then its tally has been readjusted to reflect its true score, which ranks Baz 840 behind Baz 957 with 4.5 kills and Baz 646 and Baz 802 with four kills.

## 11
### F-15B Baz 111 *Hod Ha Hanit*, Spearhead Squadron, Tel Nof, 1993

Of the 29 Baz 5 jets supplied to the IDF/AF following the second Gulf War, the pick of the bunch as far as the Israelis were concerned were the six F-15Bs that were included in this total. Prior to the arrival of these ex-USAF jets, the Baz force included just nine two-seaters – two *Peace Fox* F-15Bs, six *Peace Fox II* F-15Ds and the sole surviving *Peace Fox III* F-15D. Soon after the *Peace Fox V* jets arrived at Tel Nof, the IDF/AF received five *Peace Fox IV* F-15Ds that it had ordered several years earlier. Thus, during the course of 12 months, the total number of two-seat Bazs jets more than doubled from nine to 20, creating a substantial long-range bomber force that was eventually supplanted by the F-15I in 1998-99. Baz 111 *Hod Ha Khanit* (The Spear Head) was one of three two-seat Baz 5s assigned to the Spearhead Squadron, and it is still serving with the unit more than a decade later, albeit as a Baz AUP aircraft following its upgrade in 2002.

## 12
### F-15C Baz 575 *Maadim*, Spearhead Squadron, Tel Nof, August 1994

The Baz force has occasionally been scrambled to intercept airliners, and the jets' exploits during a handful of these missions have captured headlines. For example, on 19 September 1995, two Bazs escorted an Iranian Kish Air Boeing 707 until it landed in Israel after being hijacked, and on 28 November 2001, Baz pilots externally inspected an Arkia Boeing 757 that had narrowly escaped destruction in an SA-7 SAM attack shortly after departing the Kenyan capital Nairobi. And following the terrorist attacks on the World Trade Center in September 2001, the Tel Nof alert jets have been scrambled on numerous occasions to check the status of airliners in Israeli airspace. Two recent scrambles involved a British Airways Boeing 777 that had suffered a communication system malfunction on 26 May 2005, and an El Al Boeing 757 that was late reporting a waypoint to its air traffic controller on 19 January 2006. Undoubtedly the most famous Baz airliner 'interception' occurred on 3 August 1994, when Baz 575 was one of two F-15s that escorted a Royal Jordanian Airlines L-1011 TriStar flown by King Hussein himself – the latter had been given approval to overfly Israel as part of a recently-signed peace agreement. Baz 575 *Maadim* (Mars) was armed with four AIM-7s and four Python 3 AAMs.

## 13
### F-15I Raam 217, Hammers Squadron, Hatzerim, July 1998

When first delivered to the IDF/AF, the Raam's primary air-to-ground PGM was the LGB, and Raam 217 is depicted here in 'bomb truck' configuration. The jet is carrying three 2000-lb GBU-10s beneath its wings and fuselage, as well as 12 500-lb GBU-12s attached to the CFT pack in low drag carriage configuration. The mandatory LANTIRN navigation and targeting pods are also carried, as are two Python 4 AAMs on the wing pylons in this somewhat unorthodox mission configuration. The Hammers have subsequently added JDAM and Popeye to the Raam's air-to-ground armoury, although at this early stage in the type's service career, its arsenal was limited to LGBs and unguided bombs. Emphasising the Raam's multi-role mission capabilities, the F-15I received a scheme similar to the F-16, rather than the Baz's familiar air superiority grey. In 2005 Raam 217 became the first F-15I to be sent to the AMU for periodic depot maintenance, where engineers found it to be in excellent condition.

## 14
### F-15C Baz 818 *Tamnoon*, Spearhead Squadron, Tel Nof, July 1998

The IDF/AF celebrated its Golden Jubilee on 2 July 1998, and to mark the occasion aircraft were adorned with a special emblem throughout the Israeli Golden Jubilee Year. The IDF/AF was formally established when the State of Israel became independent on 14 May 1948, although it has its origins in the Air Service that was activated in November 1947. The first IDF/AF anniversaries were indeed celebrated during the autumn, but for many years now IDF/AF Day has been staged in the summer to coincide with the Flying School Class graduation ceremony, rather than a specific date. Baz 818 *Tamnoon* (Octopus) is depicted here with a Golden Jubilee Logo on its vertical stabilisers. The aircraft is also in 'clean' air-to-air configuration, with no external fuel tanks and only a 'light' AAM load of four Python 3 AAMs mounted on a *Magrefa* (Rake) installation, as well as two AIM-7s on the forward stations only. The jet is adorned with two 'full' kill markings, even though one of these victories was a shared success with Baz 832 – for many years IDF/AF practice was to apply only complete kill symbols. More recently, however, victory markings have been applied as accurately as possible, so Baz 818 now boasts 1.5 SyAAF roundels.

## 15

### F-15I Raam 94-0287, Hammers Squadron, Nellis AFB, Arizona, October 1998

IDF/AF aircrews participated in the USAF's *Red Flag* exercise as observers prior to the first IDF/AF jets taking part in one of these prestigious war games in October 1998. The participating F-15Is were actually factory fresh aircraft that had yet to be ferried to Israel. The jets, flown by Hammers Squadron aircrew, were painted in full IDF/AF Raam camouflage, complete with unit badges, but with USAF serials on the vertical stabilisers. 94-0287 is depicted here with no external stores bar a mandatory ACMI pod on the inner wing AAM station. Following the completion of the exercise, the aircraft was ferried to Israel in January 1999. The Hammers Squadron returned to *Red Flag* with its F-15Is in 2002 and again in 2004, ferrying its jets to and from the exercise with the support of an IDF/AF Boeing 707 tanker.

## 16

### F-15D Baz 706 *Kochav Ha Tsafon*, Spearhead Squadron, Tel Nof, November 1998

Baz 706 *Kochav Ha Tsafon* (The North Star) was the first jet to complete the Baz AUP with the Tel Nof AMU, the upgraded F-15D being rolled out in November 1998. This event coincided with the IDF/AF Jubilee, so the aircraft featured a Jubilee Logo on the outer surface of the left vertical stabiliser just above the Spearhead Squadron's badge. On the outer surface of the right stabiliser, the jet was marked with the titling *Baz AUP* in Hebrew script just below the tail number. Baz 706 is seen here in air-to-air configuration with three external fuel tanks, a CFT pack, four AIM-7s and an unusual mix of two Python 3s and two Python 4s.

## 17

### F-15I Raam 201, Flight Test Centre, Tel Nof, September 1999

The IDF/AF's FTC was involved in the Raam purchase process right from the start, with aircrew and engineers from the centre evaluating the F-16ES, the F/A-18C/D and the F-111F (the latter both in the UK and in the USA). Moshe Keret, who was FTC commander from 1992 to 1995, headed the F-15E evaluation team to the USA in November 1993. During their time in America, Israeli aircrew flew six sorties in the Strike Eagle, after which they stated that the aircraft could perform its mission in an 'impressive manner'. The FTC has a fully instrumented example of every principal frontline combat aircraft type on strength at all times, and these are primarily used for the testing and qualification of weapons and systems for frontline use. Raam 201 was actually the very first F-15I built (94-0286), completing the type's first flight from St Louis in September 1997 and then being delivered to the IDF/AF's FTC exactly two years later.

## 18

### F-15D Baz 957 *Markia Shchakim*, Spearhead Squadron, Tel Nof, September 2000

Israel initiated development of the Arrow anti-tactical ballistic missile (ATBM) long before the second Gulf War, and the impact of Iraqi SSM attacks accelerated development. The first IDF/AF Arrow ATBM battery was activated in March 2000, and development has been an ongoing process. In order to test the ATBM, and train system operators in 'real life' scenarios, the Rafael Ankor Shachor (Black Sparrow) target missile was created in the late 1990s. This large F-15-launched missile mimics the trajectory of SSMs so as to test and train both the Arrow system and the units employing it. Baz 957 *Markia Shchakim* (Sky Blazer) launched an Ankor Shachor on 14 September 2000, and the target missile was duly intercepted by a Hawk ATBM for the very first time. In 2003, IMOD Space Administration director Haim Eshed stated that Israel would possess an alternative capability for launching micro satellites weighing up to 100 kilograms 'within five years'. Eshed stated that the system relied heavily on the F-15, which could provide an on demand, cost-effective, launch capability. Possibly employing a modified Ankor Shachor, this development would give a whole new dimension to the Baz fleet's operational repertoire.

## 19

### F-15B Baz 408 *Merkevet Esh*, Double Tail Squadron, Turkey, June 2001

Israel and Turkey have mutual regional interests, which have resulted in the defence organisations from both nations establishing close ties to the point where, in early 1996, the countries signed a military cooperation agreement. A short while later, Israeli jets deployed to Turkey and Turkish fighters visited Israel to conduct training flights. IDF/AF units head to Turkish bases so that they can gain experience operating their aircraft in an unfamiliar environment, as well as to participate in the multi-nation *Anatolian Eagle* exercise. Baz 408 *Merkevet Esh* (Chariot Of Fire) deployed to a Turkish airshow at Izmir-Cigli in the summer of 2001 in a totally 'clean' configuration. Interestingly, the jet also had no cannon installed – indeed, the barrel port in the right wing root had been faired over!

## 20

### F-15I Raam 267, Hammers Squadron, RAF Waddington, UK, June-July 2001

The Raam made its first overseas deployment in the summer of 2001 when three jets (244, 267 and 269) journeyed to the UK for RAF Waddington's annual Air Tattoo. Raam 269 also participated in the flying display whilst bombed up with 12 bright orange, inert, Mk 82 LDGPs. Raam 267 was the stand out jet in respect to its markings, as it featured the first iteration of a proposed Hammers unit emblem on the outer surfaces of its vertical stabilisers. This particular artwork was not endorsed by the squadron hierarchy, and it was removed shortly after the jet returned to Israel.

## 21

### F-15B Baz 113 *Zeev Boded*, Double Tail Squadron, Tel Nof, September 2001

The Double Tail Squadron celebrated 25 years of F-15 operations in September 2001, and Baz 113 *Zeev Boded* (Lone Wolf), which had just completed the AUP, became synonymous with this event thanks to a series of air-to-air photographs that were taken at the time. The aircraft was specially loaded in an air combat configuration for the photo-shoot, boasting four AIM-7s and four Python 4 AAMs, as well as a single centreline external fuel tank. It was also marked with *Baz AUP* titling in Hebrew script just below the tail number, although it lacked the tail art associated with upgraded jets that was introduced in its definite form from 2002. Many Baz 5 F-15s have their USAF serials painted in small digits at the base of the vertical stabilisers, including Baz 113 (73-0113).

## 22

### F-15D Baz 701 *Shual Ha Esh*, Spearhead Squadron, Tel Nof, June 2002

The Spearhead Squadron celebrated 20 years of Baz operations in June 2002, and in order to mark the occasion, Baz 701 *Shual Ha Esh* (The Fire Fox) conducted a dedicated air-to-air photographic session. The unit is suitably proud of its precision strike capability, so it loaded the jet up with a CFT-II pack, a Popeye affixed to its left wing pylon and the ASM's datalink pod under the fuselage. The jet is depicted here with the definitive Baz AUP tail art that was also introduced in 2002. Note also that the jet's radome has been painted in a darker shade of grey.

## 23

### F-15I Raam 246, Hammers Squadron, Hatzerim, August 2003

Hammers Squadron Raam 246 was adorned with the unit's definitive tail art in August 2003. This version was very similar in overall shape to the first iteration worn by Raam 267 in the summer of 2001, but it was larger and more colourful. Applying such a large and complex piece of artwork such as this has taken a long time, and only a few Hammers' jets (Raam 212, 220, 234, 252 and 271) were painted in 2004-05.

## 24

### F-15D Baz 280 *Yad Ha Nefetz*, Double Tail Squadron, Tel Nof, September 2004

Baz 280 *Yad Ha Nefetz* (Shutter Hand) was the last F-15 to undergo the AMU Baz AUP, being rolled out in November 2005. In this artwork, the jet is equipped with CFTs and armed with four AIM-7s and four Python 4 AAMs. Of greatest interest is the rarely photographed reconnaissance pod (mounted to the centreline pylon) that can generate digital images and send them to a ground station via a datalink. The jet is adorned with a GBU-15 kill marking dating back to the October 1985 mission to Tunis, as well as the nosecone tip painted in a darker shade of grey.

# BIBLIOGRAPHY

**Aloni, Shlomo,** 'The Fighting Baz', Air Forces Monthly issue 55, p37-40, October 1992

**Aloni, Shlomo,** 'Syrian shootdown', Air Forces Monthly issue 143, p32-34, February 2000

**Aloni, Shlomo,** Osprey Combat Aircraft 23 *Arab-Israeli Air Wars 1947-82*, Osprey Publishing, 2001

**Aloni, Shlomo,** 'Thunder from the Negev', Air Pictorial volume 63 No 9, p676-678, September 2001

**Aloni, Shlomo,** 'Israeli F-15 upgrade: Improving the Baz', International Air Power Review volume 4, p30-31, May 2002

**Aloni, Shlomo,** 'Israeli Thunder', Air Forces Monthly issue179, p52-56, February 2003

**Ball, Ray,** Camouflage & Markings No 4 *The Israeli Air Force Part 2, 1967 to 2001*, Guideline Publications, 2001

**Borovik, Yehuda,** Warbirds Illustrated No 23 *Israeli Air Force,* Arms and Armour Press, 1984

**Claire, Rodger W,** *Raid on the Sun*, Broadway Books, 2004

**Cohen, Eliezer,** *Israel's Best Defense*, Airlife, 1993

**Efrati, Yoav,** *Colors & Markings of The Israeli Air Force*, IsraDecal Publications, 2005

**Gresham, John D,** 'F-15 Eagle Variants Briefing', World Air Power Journal Volume 33 p114-137, Summer 1998

**Gunston, Bill,** *An Illustrated Guide to the Israeli Air Force*, Salamander Books 1982

**Handleman, Philip,** *Mid-East Aces*, Osprey Publishing, 1991

**Lapidot, Aharon and Merav Halperin,** *G-Suit*, Sphere Books, 1990

**McKinnon, Dan,** *Bullseye One Reactor*, Airlife Publishing, 1988

**Mersky, Peter B,** *Israeli Fighter Aces*, Specialty Press, 1997

**Nicolle, David and Tom Cooper,** Osprey Combat Aircraft 44 *Arab MiG-19 and MiG-21 Units in Combat*, Osprey Publishing, 2004

**Nordeen, Lon,** *Fighters Over Israel*, Orion Books, 1990

**Norton, Bill,** *Air War on the Edge*, Midland Publishing, 2004

**Weiss, Raanan,** *Aircraft in Detail: F-15I Raam in IAF service*, IsraDecal Publications, 2006

**Yonai, Ehud,** *No Margin for Error*, Pantheon Press, 1993

**Zidon, Ofer and Shlomo Aloni,** *Fly With The Israeli Air Force*, Wizard Publications (Israel), 2004

**Zidon, Ofer and Shlomo Aloni,** *Israeli Air Force Yearbook 2005*, Wizard Publications (Israel), 2005

# INDEX

References to illustrations are shown in **bold**. Plates are shown with page and caption locators in brackets.